ANIMALS IN AMERICAN FOLK ART

ANIMALS IN AMERICAN FOLK ART

WENDY LAVITT

Alfred A. Knopf

NEW YORK

1990

THIS IS A BORZOI BOOK
PUBLISHED BY ALFRED A. KNOPF, INC.

Copyright © 1990 by Wendy Lavitt

LIBRARY OF CONGRESS
CATALOGING-IN-PUBLICATION DATA

Lavitt, Wendy.
    Animals in American folk art / Wendy Lavitt. — 1st ed.
       p.   cm.
    Includes bibliographical references.
    ISBN 0-394-57156-8
    1. Folk art—United States.   2. Animals in art. I. Title.
NK805.L38
745'.0973—dc20   89-71695
                                                          CIP

Composed by New England Typographic Service, Inc.,
Bloomfield, Connecticut
Color separations by Reprocolor Llovet, Barcelona
Printed and bound by Cayfosa, Barcelona
Designed by Peter A. Andersen

Manufactured in Spain
First Edition

FRONTISPIECE:
"Jack's Box". Anonymous. Watercolor under glass box lid.
12" x 7½". 1862. "Pookeepsie," N.Y. Courtesy of Lillian and
Jerry Grossman. Photograph: Edward Shoffstall

FOR MEL, KATHY, JOHN, AND MEREDITH,
AND OUR FAVORITE ANIMALS, AMBER, MOCHA, AND ALFIE

Blue Jays. Bernier. Polychromed wood and metal. 10½″ length and 10¾″ length. 1900–10.
Saco-Biddeford, Maine. Courtesy of Barbara Johnson, Esq. Photograph: Clem Fiori

CONTENTS

ACKNOWLEDGMENTS

FROM THE INCEPTION of *Animals in American Folk Art* to the last word and photograph I have been overwhelmed by the enthusiasm and generosity of collectors, galleries, private dealers, and museum personnel—all of whom have made suggestions, provided objects to be photographed, and given of themselves and their time. The eagerness with which people helped me made working on this book a joy. A special note to Alice Quinn, whose guidance and ideas were invaluable, and heartfelt thanks to Vicky Wilson, my editor. I would also like to thank the following individuals and institutions:

The Abrahams, Judith Alexander, American Classics—Meryl Weiss, American Museum of Natural History, Ames Gallery of Folk Art, Marna Anderson, Aarne Anton, Joshua Baer, Bennington Museum, Robert Bishop, the late Robert Bonner, Dr. Robert Booth, Robert Cargo Folk Art Gallery, Cavin-Morris Gallery, Will Channing, the Clokeys, Colonial Williamsburg Foundation, Colorado Historical Association, Columbia County Historical Society, Suzanne Courcier and Robert Williams, Jordan Davis, Mary Davis, Denver Art Museum, Jeannine Dobbs, Nancy Druckman, Lee and Joseph Dumas, Leslie Eisenberg, Epstein-Powell Gallery, M. Finkel and Daughter, Janet Fleisher Gallery, F. Barrie Freeman Antiques, Ron Fritz, Peter T. Furst, Patty Gagarin, Gasperi Folk Art Gallery, Sidney Gecker, Lillian and Jerry Grossman, Larry Hackley, Julie Hall, Kenneth Hammitt, Maureen and David Haska, Bert Hemphill, Willie Mae Hentz, Hillman-Gemini Antiques, Hirschl & Adler Folk, Elaine Horwitch, Stephen Huneck, Barbara

Johnson, Jay Johnson, Kentucky Art and Craft Foundation, Phylis Kind Gallery, June Lambert Antiques, Marston Luce, Laura Luckey, *Maine Antiques Digest,* Kenneth and Ida Manko, Luella McCloud, Memorial Art Gallery of the University of Rochester, MESDA, MIA Gallery, Frank Miele, Steve Miller, Bettie Mintz, Morning Star Gallery, El Museo del Barrio, Museum of American Folk Art, Newark Museum, New York State Historical Association, Olde Hope Antiques, John Ollman, Oregon Historical Society, Samuel Pennington, Lynda D. Peters, Inc., Philadelphia Museum of Art, Sergio and Penny Prosperpi, Randall and Koblenz, Susan and Sy Rapaport, Richard Rasso, Roger Ricco and Frank Maresca, Sheila and Edwin Rideout, Marguerite Riordan, the Robertsons, Sue Rosen, Luise Ross, Stella Rubin, Saint Augustine Historical Society, Betty and Joel Schatzberg, Kathy Schoemer, David Schorsch, Stephen Score, Richard Sears, Tony and Marie Shank, Edward Shoffstall, Robert W. Skinner, Inc., Sanford Smith, Smith Gallery, Sotheby's, Edward L. Steckler, Sterling & Hunt, Tartt Gallery, William Tellini, Frederick I. Thaler, Walowen & Schneider, Willis Henry Auctions, Brian Windsor, Edith Wise.

Painted Box
Rufus Cole (b. 1804)
Painted wood
5¾″ x 13½″
c. 1830
Mayfield, Fulton County, N.Y.
Courtesy of Robert W. Skinner, Inc., Boston, Mass.

Rufus Cole, an artist best known for his painted clock cases, decorated the top of this wooden box with a freehand painting of a pair of rabbits amid luxuriant foliage.

ANIMALS IN AMERICAN FOLK ART

Garden of Eden Overmantle. Anonymous. Oil on poplar panel. 28″ x 37″. c. 1800–1825.
Massachusetts. Collection of Robert and Katherine Booth. Photograph courtesy of David A.
Schorsch, New York City

Inspired by a Brueghel painting.

INTRODUCTION

FROM PREY TO PET the legacy of animals in American folk art has been both enduring and lively. Next to ourselves, animals are the most frequently depicted subjects in folk art. Whether guardians of the hearth, faithful companions, or creatures of the wild, animals, birds, fish, reptiles, and insects have preoccupied our thoughts since the days of exploration. Early travelers illustrated maps, globes, letters, and journals with the animals of the New World. They were followed by succeeding generations who paid homage to animals in a number of ways. During the Revolution the rattlesnake stood for the fighting spirit of the patriots, inspiring the popular slogan: "Don't tread on me." After a brief flurry of interest in the wild turkey, the eagle was chosen as the symbol of the new nation.

Folk artists of the eighteenth and nineteenth centuries lived surrounded by animals on farms and in nearby fields and forests, observing many species on a firsthand basis. While some drew their inspiration from daily life, others pored over periodicals and books, dreaming of animals in faraway places. Not surprisingly, people's reasons for creating animal folk art were as varied as the animals themselves. Whatever the motive, the result was an endearing procession of creatures in many forms. Whether realistic or abstract, whimsical or serious, all exhibited the spark of originality and freshness.

One traditional function of the folk artist has been to record the mundane, filtering it through his personal lens. The prosperity of nineteenth-century American farmers can be seen through the many portraits of prized livestock. An out-

Mr. & Mrs. John Griswold
Salting Sheep
James E. Johnson
(1810–1858)
Oil on canvas
85¼'' x 49''
c. 1837
Spencertown, N.Y.
Courtesy of the Columbia
County Historical Society

James E. Johnson was
commissioned to paint the
Griswolds on their estate.
Mr. Griswold, a wool
merchant, naturally wished
to be shown with his pride
and joy—his livestock.

Horse Hooked Rug
Anonymous
Wool and cotton on burlap
56″ x 31″
Late 19th century
New England
Courtesy of Elliott and
Grace Snyder,
South Egremont, Mass.

"Blue Hill Hotel" Sign
Anonymous
Painted wood
30″ x 40½″
c. 1809–87
Milton, Mass.
Private collection
Photograph courtesy of the
Bennington Museum

This sign advertises Samuel
and Joshua Tucker's hotel,
built in 1809 on the newly
laid "Blue Hill Turnpike" in
Milton, Massachusetts.

Turkey Coverlet
Anonymous
Wool
84″ square
c. 1876
Pennsylvania
Courtesy of Maureen and
David Haska

An unusual Centennial
coverlet celebrating the wild
turkey—also a possible
symbol, along with the eagle,
of the United States. The
building on the border
appears to be Philadelphia
Hall, home of the 1876
Exposition.

pouring of paintings by mostly anonymous artists celebrating their beloved pets and barnyard companions reflected the value accorded domestic animals. Painters, including America's beloved Edward Hicks, eagerly accepted commissions to paint neighbors' livestock. A receipt on the back of a Hicks canvas states:

James Cornell to Edward Hicks De To Painting his Prize Bull. $15.00 Rec 5th mo 16th 1846 the above in full of all demands by me. E. Hicks.

The bull commissioned by a proud farmer proclaimed his success. The dog who added a touch of warmth to an otherwise somber painting would not be so utilized by today's folk painters, but in the nineteenth century such a device appears to have been taken for granted among New England painters and their sitters.

The folk artist also documented rapidly changing ways of life, especially the vanishing frontier. Animals such as the bison and the wild horse were vividly portrayed by those on the scene. While many folk artists were preoccupied with the frontier, animals in the East that were destined to disappear were also depicted. The charming Carolina Parakeets, so well known in Pennsylvania German folk art, were extinct by 1914 as a result of needless slaughter by hunters. However, their frequent appearance on show towels, frakturs, and samplers ensured them a kind of immortality.

Cat with Mouse Painting
Anonymous
Watercolor on paper
17½″ x 20″
19th century
Courtesy of Mr. and Mrs.
Kenneth Hammitt
Photograph: Ray Scoury

A good mouser was a valued
member of the family,
and was often immortalized
in paint.

The colonists displayed an avid curiosity about rare beasts, and traveling exhibitions of exotic animals commanded the attention of entire towns. Artists often relied upon engravings found in books in order to more accurately depict camels, tigers, giraffes, monkeys, and other creatures so fascinating to townspeople who rarely traveled more than thirty miles from home.

Contemporary folk artists living in a world of mass communication are not depicting wild animals for the edification of their audiences. Their concerns center on personal visions and their need to express what they wish to say about a particular animal or species. Even though the threads between contemporary folk artists and their predecessors might appear tenuous, there exists an invisible tie, binding them together in a mutual interest. Whether working today or in years past, many artists feel compelled to depict animals as part of a spiritual plan, to define animals in terms of the human condition, or to capture their essence simply for the love of it.

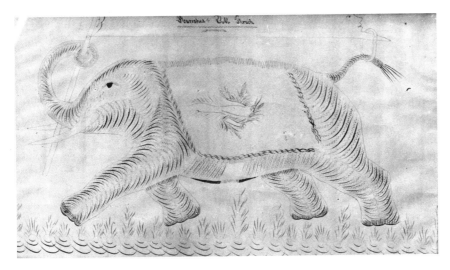

Elephant
Calligraphy—"Flourished"
B. M. Thrush
Ink on paper
18″ x 36″
19th century
Courtesy of Sidney and
Sandra Gecker

"Pikes Peak or Bust"
Alex Comparet
Oil on canvas
18″ x 24″
1870
Colorado Territory
Courtesy of Colorado
Historical Society

It has been said that the ox
rather than the horse is
responsible for the success of
the westward movement, for
it was the ox, the beast of
burden, who shouldered the
heavy loads across the plains.

The Ox "Pennsylvania"
Anonymous
Oil on canvas
29¼″ x 23½″
1841
Berks County, Pa.
Courtesy of
Barbara Johnson, Esq.
Photograph: Clem Fiori

The ox "Pennsylvania"
weighed a record 3,350
pounds and was eight years
old when painted. His owner
was so proud of him that the
painter has depicted the
animal twice—once standing
and once sitting.

Lydia Boden Sampler. Lydia Boden. Marblehead School of Needlework.
Silk on linen. 10¾″ x 8½″. c. 1788. Marblehead, Mass. Collection of
G. W. Samaha. Photograph courtesy of David A. Schorsch, New York City

Animals in samplers are often small and insignificant. In this example, the
cat and birds are unusually large. Only two samplers are known from the
Marblehead School of Needlework in Massachusetts.

Young Girl with Cat Painting. Anonymous. Oil on canvas in original painted frame. 23″ x 18″. c. 1840. New England. Courtesy of Olde Hope Antiques, New Hope, Pa.

Many itinerant folk painters portrayed children as old men and women. Here the tiny kitten's wizened face is in keeping with the portrait of the child.

Homestead of Joseph Wienz
Probably Sarah Wienz
(his daughter)
Tempera on linen
24″ x 30″
Dated 1892
Eastern New York State
Courtesy of Olde Hope
Antiques, New Hope, Pa.

Mourning Fob with Portrait
of Cow
Anonymous
Watercolor on ivory, hair,
and silver
10½″ x 1⅝″ x ⅜″
19th century
Courtesy of the Museum of
American Folk Art

THE EIGHTEENTH AND NINETEENTH CENTURIES

In the Beginning

LONG BEFORE the Europeans arrived in the New World, prehistoric artists depicted the animals who shared the continent with them. Petroglyphs, decorated pottery, bone sculptures, and wood carvings tell of the first Americans' artistic preoccupation with the animal kingdom. In cave paintings artists tried to symbolize an animal and capture its essence. Symbols proclaimed the power—both physical and spiritual—of the prolific wildlife found in all parts of the land and surrounding seas.

Archeological finds at various sites bear witness to the many animals depicted by anonymous prehistoric artists. At the snaketown mounds (southeast of present-day Phoenix, Arizona) excavations produced whole menageries of tiny clay animals.[1] At a Pueblo Grande site in Arizona, a ceremonial burial site yielded a mysterious cache of pottery—twenty-three bighorn sheep. No one knows whether they represented the animal kingdom or were objects of worship.[2] Who was the first Mimbres potter in southwestern New Mexico to create a black-and-white story bowl decorated with elegantly stylized animals? The innovations of prehistoric man will always produce more questions than can be answered.

The prehistoric communities knew animals as hunters and prey—powerful creatures upon whom men depended for survival. Hunting the larger animals required strategies worthy of modern-day military maneuvers—all the able-bodied men of a tribe needed to be actively involved in stampeding, herding, slaughtering, and hauling. Deer and buffalo meat were supplemented with rabbit,

OPPOSITE PAGE:
Portrait of a Girl in Pink with Cat
Zedekiah Belknap
(1781–1858)
Oil on canvas
28″ x 24″
c. 1825–1830
New England
Collection of Robert and Katherine Booth
Photograph courtesy of David A. Schorsch,
New York City

The cat "standing" beside its mistress looks demonic. Note the object on the little girl's lap: a popular Pennsylvania German squeak toy with pigeons on the base.

Effigy Pipe
Hopewell Mounds
Stone
4½″ x 2″
C. 100 B.C.–A.D. 600
Courtesy of the American
Museum of Natural History,
Neg. #291278

This effigy pipe depicts a
spoonbill duck on a fish.

prairie chicken, beaver, and other small animals. Dangerous confrontations with
wild animals were all the more terrifying due to the primitive conditions in caring
for the wounded and ill. The elements of fear and power—integral features of
primitive religions—were partly responsible for a mythic regard for animals.
Appearing frequently in ancient American art are images of animals drawn from
sacred tenets, anthropomorphic beliefs, and shaman-inspired imaginings. Dreamlike renditions of animals can be seen throughout American Indian mythology.

When the Europeans arrived, an artistic expression based upon realism appeared. Artists accompanying the first expeditions duly recorded the fauna and
flora for their patrons. They saw a virgin land abounding with prolific wildlife.
Species destined to be extinct in a few centuries were documented by the art of
young America.

Adoration of the Magi
Attributed to J. Cooper
Oil on canvas
30¼″ x 25¼″
Probably New York City,
C. 1735
Courtesy of Mattatuck
Museum, Waterbury, Conn.

One of the earliest known
paintings by an American
artist to include animals.

The settlement of the colonies, the reliance upon agrarian communities, and the subsequent trail of western expansion necessarily included domestication of animals. In becoming valued property, animals were portrayed in paintings as a reflection of their owners' prosperity. Wealth and its accoutrements have always been a part of the art world, stimulating commissions and often dictating the subject matter of major works. In America, well-to-do colonists wanted portraits of their family and prized livestock. Paintings of children frequently included pets who subtly reflected the household's status. Indeed, birds, cats, and dogs, along with toys, jewelry, and elegant clothing, were indications of a genteel lifestyle. The inclusion of pets in an otherwise stilted portraiture was not lost on itinerant artists who needed to divert attention away from an awkward pose or a leaden face. In most instances unschooled artists had less trouble portraying animals than people, and it is not unusual to find a realistic rendering of a dog or cat next to a rather stiff figure of a child. The flat, simplified animal that often possesses an innocent appeal is today appreciated as folk art.

"Birdsey Hall"
Residence Sign
Anonymous
Painted wood with
iron brackets
50″ x 25½″
1804–10
Goshen, Conn.
Courtesy of Olde Hope
Antiques, New Hope, Pa.

Birdsey Hall, for which this
sign was made, was built by
Birdsey Norton in 1804 and
was one of the most notable
brick houses in the state.

American Woolen Sign
Anonymous
Painted wood
36″ x 24″
c. 1900
Providence, R.I.
Courtesy of Allan Katz

Trade Signs, Weathervanes, and Grave Markers

EARLY DEPICTIONS of animals were not limited to paintings. Sculpture in the form of weathervanes, utilitarian objects, trade signs, and even grave markers appears as early as the eighteenth century. Because of the low rate of literacy, tradespeople needed to reach the entire population with images rather than print. Therefore, a three-dimensional fish might be used for a fish market while a figure of a lion, eagle, or cock would announce an inn. By the eighteenth century signs proliferated in towns along the eastern seaboard. Most of the early signs were three-dimensional, created by the local wood carvers. As the literacy rate rose, flat signs with printing gradually replaced the more time-consuming sculptural signs. Since artists often supplemented meager incomes by sign painting, ship figure carving, and other occupations utilizing their highly developed skills, the quality of early signs and their ilk can be remarkable. Surprisingly, not everyone appreciated the work of these artists. An article in a colonial newspaper, *The Spectator,* in 1710 decried what it considered a motley assortment of animals portrayed on various signs:

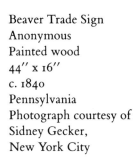

Beaver Trade Sign
Anonymous
Painted wood
44″ x 16″
c. 1840
Pennsylvania
Photograph courtesy of
Sidney Gecker,
New York City

Partridge Trade Sign
Anonymous
Wrought iron and
painted metal
25½″ x 27″
Early 19th century
Probably New England
Courtesy of Mr. and Mrs.
Kenneth Hammitt
Photograph: Ray Scoury

Our streets are filled with blue boars, black swans, and red lions; not to mention flying pigs, and hogs in armour, with many other creatures more extraordinary than any in the deserts of Africa.[3]

A few early trade signs were combinations of imagery and print. One New England tavern boasted a sign of an eagle hovering over a hen with a brood of chicks. The eagle held a crown in its beak bearing the patriotic inscription: "May the Wings of Liberty cover the Chickens of Freedom, and pluck the Crown from the Enemy's Head."[4] Another New England sign hung on the Goodwin Tavern in the early nineteenth century, featuring a rather tame-looking lion in chains. The artist, unlike most sign painters, signed his name, "William Rice." While many eighteenth-century signs depicted the English lion, a number of the crowns were painted over after the Revolution.

In early gravestone art, animals embodied religious tenets and symbols. Very little is known about the early gravestone artists, but one carver signed his work "J.N." in Quincy, Massachusetts, in 1703. He is believed to be the first New Eng-

Lamb Figure
Attributed to John Bell
(1800–1880)
Glazed stoneware
11″ x 2½″
c. 1850
Waynesboro, Pa.
Courtesy of Sidney Gecker,
New York City

When used as grave markers,
lamb figures usually were
unglazed or merely covered
with white slip. This rare
glazed figure of a lamb might
have been used as a doorstop,
an ornament, or a marker.

land carver to use peacocks for a marker.[5] The peacock symbolized incorruptibility of the flesh. The most common animal markers included the rooster (repentance), the dove (the soul or cross of redemption), and the eagle (transporter of the soul). Less frequently seen were butterflies emerging from their cocoons, signifying spiritual purification and transformation. However, gravestone art was not destined to be a popular art form, and it wasn't until the appearance of handmade weathervanes in the mid-seventeenth century that the era of affordable sculpture had its nascence.

The earliest documented American weathervane in the shape of a creature is a cockerel made by Shem Drowne (1683–1774) for the New Brick Church of Boston, Massachusetts, in 1721. A fitting image for the times, the cock, long a Christian symbol, also heralded the dawning of a new day—a new world. However, another vane by Shem Drowne, a grasshopper for Faneuil Hall in Boston (1742), had for centuries symbolized the market or marketplace in Europe. The son of Shem Drowne, Thomas Drowne (1715–1796), continued his father's business of

Sheep Sculpture
Anonymous
Soapstone
3½″ x 5″ x 1½″
c. 1825
New England
Courtesy of F. Barrie
Freeman Antiques,
West Bath, Maine

This carving was found in a
trunk in a New England
attic, where it had lain
undiscovered for years. The
"1785" inscription on the
base of the carving remains a
mystery since the sculpture is
thought to date from the
early 19th century.

repairing and making weathervanes. Apparently inheriting his father's talents, he was well known for his weathercocks, which he formed using the patterns handed down from father to son. His vanes could be bought for modest sums—in 1771, "a cock . . . gilt in the best manner" cost £12.[6]

The weathercock, a familiar sight in eighteenth-century New England towns, became a recognizable landmark, an icon of village life to which Henry Wadsworth Longfellow paid homage in *Paul Revere's Ride:*

> *It was one by the village clock*
> *When he galloped into Lexington.*
> *He saw the gilded weathercock*
> *Swim in the moonlight as he passed . . .*

In the nineteenth century a panoply of domestic animals appeared alongside the weathercock. The primitive iron or wooden vanes gave way to zinc and copper weathervanes from manufacturers who offered a large choice through their catalogues. While the horse became a best-seller, cows, pigs, sheep, and goats—the backbone of a farmer's livelihood—were well represented by weathervanes that were deemed appropriate decoration for the elaborate barns of the late nineteenth century. Examples representing successful breeds such as the Merino or the Cotswold sheep were attractive to farmers owning such prize-winning lines. Because

Reindeer Vane
Anonymous
Sheet iron
24″ x 27½″
1850–80
New Hampshire
Courtesy of
Lynda D. Peters, Inc.,
Scituate, R.I.

Rooster Weathervane
Anonymous
Sheet iron
26″ x 21″
1850–80
Pennsylvania
Courtesy of
Lynda D. Peters, Inc.,
Scituate, R.I.

Rooster Weathervane
Anonymous
Sheet iron
38⅝″ x 26¾″
c. 1860
Bucks County, Pa.
Courtesy of Hirschl &
Adler Folk, New York City

Fish Weathervane
Anonymous
Wrought iron and copper
35½″ x 7¼″
1800–50
Courtesy of Artvest
Collection

This weathervane has an almost abstract, modern beauty in its form.

sheep were not imported to America in large numbers until the 1870s, they were not reproduced as often in weathervanes as the horse.

By the late nineteenth century dairying had become one of the largest industries. Dairy farms specializing in a particular breed would often choose the farm's weathervane to advertise it. Cow and bull vanes of specific breeds, while first commissioned by individual farmers, were then reused by the manufacturer, who not only kept the costly iron mold but also added a new model to his catalogue. Other industries that could be represented by an animal vane, such as the wool mills of New England, ordered them from weathervane manufacturers' catalogues.

Even with competition from an expanding line of vanes, the weathercock held its own in popularity. Weathervane manufacturers designed series of gilded, full-bodied roosters that were more realistic-looking than their predecessors. Today when many Americans think of a weathervane, their first image is of the rooster atop a New England barn.

Flying Horse Weathervane
A. L. Jewell & Co.
Gilt, sheet metal, and zinc
32″ x 35″
Late 19th century
Waltham, Mass.
Courtesy of Hirschl &
Adler Folk, New York City

Bee Weathervane
Anonymous
Wrought iron and wood
21½″ length
Early 20th century
Eastern seaboard
Courtesy of
Frederic I. Thaler,
Cromwell Bridge, Conn.

Although the bee as a symbol
of industry has a long history
as a trade motif, it makes an
unusual weathervane.

Dolphin Weathervane
J. W. Fiske Co.
Copper with original gold
paint and verdigris
38″ x 24″
c. 1880
New York City
Courtesy of
Lynda D. Peters, Inc.,
Scituate, R.I.

The dolphin, a well-known
symbol in ancient Greece and
medieval heraldry, became a
popular motif during the
Greek Revival movement in
America (1830–40).

Hen Weathervane
James Lombard (b. 1865)
Wood and metal
17¾″ x 21″
1885–90
Bridgton, Maine
Courtesy of the New York
State Historical Association,
Cooperstown

Lombard's sculptural
weathervanes, with their
distinctive tail feathers, were
sought after by neighboring
farmers. Today his weathercocks are lauded for their
design and collected by
museums.

Pig Weathervane. Anonymous. Tin. Dimensions unavailable.
Late 19th century. Courtesy of Marna Anderson

By the late 19th century, a wide range of manufactured
weathervanes were available through mail-order catalogues and
stores, but people still preferred to make their own. Here the
maker chose to use tin for his weathervane instead of copper
or iron.

Cotswold Ram Weathervane. L. W. Cushing & Co. Molded copper.
32½″ x 39½″. c. 1880. Waltham, Mass. Courtesy of Hirschl & Adler Folk,
New York City

A number of weathervane manufacturers listed rams in their inventory,
including the Marino and the Cotswold breeds.

Rooster Weathervane
Anonymous
Painted and carved wood
19″ x 26″
19th century
Massachusetts
Photograph courtesy of
Sidney Gecker,
New York City

This weathervane was
probably made by a local
farmer.

Rooster and Hen
Weathervane
Anonymous
Carved wood with
applied wings
29½″ x 11¼″
c. 1900–20
Lancaster County, Pa.
Courtesy of Olde Hope
Antiques, New Hope, Pa.
Collection of Joseph and
Janet Visokay

Dove Weathervane
Anonymous
Sheet metal
16″ x 12″
19th century
Eastern seaboard
Courtesy of Bettie Mintz,
"All of Us Americans"
Folk Art Gallery,
Bethesda, Md.

This beautiful sheet-iron
silhouette possesses a gentleness not often associated
with weathervanes.

Fox Weathervane
Anonymous
Cast iron
30″ length
c. 1880s
New Hampshire
Private collection
Photograph courtesy of
Kenneth and Ida Manko,
Moody, Maine

One of the more unusual
subjects for a weathervane
(the fox appealed to hunters),
as is the vane of a dog in
pursuit of a frightened fox.

Tavern Sign. Anonymous. Oil on panel. 27″ x 22½″. 19th century.
Pennsylvania. Courtesy of the Westmoreland Museum of Art

A seemingly modern portrait of a lion. The open, friendly expression is rare
in a 19th-century sign.

Eagle Sculpture
Anonymous
Carved poplar
47″ x 30″
19th century
Courtesy of Hirschl &
Adler Folk, New York City

The fierce stance of this eagle
is typical of 19th-century
professional carvers (the folky
parrotlike eagles were usually
made by amateurs).

Eagles

As America's favorite symbol, the weathercock was superseded by the eagle,
whose designation as the national emblem by the Continental Congress in 1782
assured its popularity for over fifty years. Ironically, Benjamin Franklin preferred
the wild turkey, which he considered to be "A much more respectable Bird and a
true Native of America. . . . He is a bird of courage and would not hesitate to
Attack a grenadier of the British Guards."[7] Franklin was overruled and the eagle
was incorporated not only in official seals but into ordinary contexts running the
gauntlet from coverlets to whiskey jugs. Even George Washington succumbed to
eagle mania, ordering eagle buttons for his jacket.[8] He was moved by the sight of
silhouetted eagles on whitewashed front windows of homes lining the route of his
tour of the colonies in 1789. The eagle personified America and thus became a
favorite subject for the craftsmen of the day.

Nathaniel Hawthorne's tale *The Bald Eagle,* concerning Lafayette's triumphal

Temperance Victory Eagle
Anonymous
Watercolor on cut paper
7¾″ x 12¼″
c. 1830–50
New York State
Courtesy of the New York
Historical Association,
Cooperstown

The most elaborate forms
of scherenschnitte (called
schnibbele, or cuttings, in
Pennsylvania, where they
were most popular) were
made by schoolmasters and
given to students as a reward
for excellence.

tour of America in 1824, takes place in a tavern in the Connecticut Valley. The
entrance to this famous tavern is described in these words:

Before the door stood a tall yellow signpost, from which hung a white sign embla-
zoned with a fierce bald eagle, holding an olive branch in one claw, and a flash of
forked lightning in the other. Underneath was written in large black letters, "THE
BALD EAGLE: GOOD ENTERTAINMENT FOR MAN AND BEAST: by Jonathan Dew-
lap, Esq."

The most famous American carver of eagles, John Haley Bellamy (1836–1914),
endowed his sculptures with the vitality and movement synonymous with great
folk art. Originally from Kittery Point, Maine, Bellamy apprenticed in Charles-
town, Massachusetts, in 1857, where he became known for his graceful yet bold
renditions of America's favorite symbol. His many commissions for the Charles-
town and Boston Navy Yards included a monumental carved figurehead for
the USS *Lancaster.* He established his own shop, employing workers who carved
and assembled eagles that could number one hundred in a single order. In addition
to sculptures in-the-round, Bellamy specialized in "emblematic frames and
brackets." Although many of his plaques bear standard patriotic slogans, several
amusing plaques designed as "greeting cards" included banners with bold calligra-

phic script expressing such sentiments as "Remember the *Maine,*" "Happy Birthday," and "Merry Christmas." Bellamy, like many folk artists, wore numerous hats (inventor, poet, journalist, sculptor) and also like many artists battled with bouts of depression and alcoholism. In his last years he was known to walk to Portsmouth with a carving under his arm and return with a bottle of whiskey.[9]

Eagle Sculpture
Anonymous
Painted wood with glass eyes
25¼″ x 13″
Early 19th century
Pennsylvania
Courtesy of Mr. and Mrs.
Kenneth Hammitt
Photograph: Ray Scoury

The unknown Pennsylvania artist who carved this imposing eagle preferred to emphasize the contours of the bird rather than its feathers.

Eagle Plaque
John Haley Bellamy
(1836–1914)
Painted pine
38″ length
Late 19th century
Kittery, Maine
Courtesy of
Maine Antiques Digest

One of Bellamy's many
eagle plaques with painted
"greeting card" sentiments.
"DIRIGO" is the motto of
Maine.

Eagle
Anonymous
Carved pine with traces of
weathered paint
21″ x 11″
c. 1830–40
Gray Station, Tenn.
Courtesy of Richard and
Betty Ann Rasso,
East Chatham, N.Y.

One of a pair of gable-end
ornaments from a
19th-century home.

Horse Trade Sign
Anonymous
Sheet iron with traces of
polychrome
37″ x 33″
c. 1870
Pennsylvania
Courtesy of Hirschl &
Adler Folk, New York City

Horses

IF THE EAGLE expressed America's official pride, the horse joyfully proclaimed its pleasure and progress. Horses not only were an integral part of the colonial economy, they also provided life's lighter moments in the form of horse racing. Although officially frowned on, horse racing was avidly followed throughout the colonies. A typical racetrack was described in 1670:

> Toward the middle of Long Island lyeth a plain sixteen miles long and four broad —where you shall find neither stick nor stone to hinder the horses heels, or endanger them in their races, and once a year the best Horses in the Island are brought hither to try their swiftness, and the swift is rewarded with a silver cup.[10]

Portraits of racehorses, engravings, and numerous weathervanes celebrating America's favorite trotters attest to the popularity of the sport. The horse was also

Horse Watercolor
Anonymous
Watercolor on glass
15″ x 13″
1860s
Pennsylvania
Courtesy of Brian Windsor
Antiques, Staten Island, N.Y.,
and Victoria Wilson
Photograph:
Edward Shoffstall

Note the tramp art frame.

Horse Painting
Anonymous
Oil on canvas
19″ x 13″
19th century
Courtesy of Sterling & Hunt,
Long Island, N.Y.
Photograph:
Edward Shoffstall

Horse Hooked Rug
Anonymous
Wool on burlap
29″ x 43″
19th century
Courtesy of Stephen Score,
Essex, Mass.
Photograph:
Edward Shoffstall

Horse Pulltoy
Anonymous
Wood with leather ears
13½″ x 11½″
c. 1860
Courtesy of Hillman-Gemini
Antiques, New York City
Photograph:
Edward Shoffstall

appreciated for less spectacular characteristics: his strength and endurance as a plow horse and as an essential means of transportation. Country painters often immortalized a favorite horse and even included toy horses in their portraits of children.

Toy horses and rocking horses were so popular in paintings and sculpture that they comprise a category in themselves. As early as 1785 a Philadelphia cabinetmaker advertised: "Rocking-horses in the neatest and best manner to teach children to ride and give them a wholesome and pleasing exercise."[11] The fact that skilled cabinetmakers often made rocking horses partially accounts for the artistry of many such horses made in the eighteenth and nineteenth centuries. Occasionally, the trade of the maker is evidenced in the product, as in one example made by a chairmaker that stands on simple turned legs supported by stretchers.[12] Some rocking horses were sturdy wooden constructions resembling rowboats. It is known that carvers of ship figureheads sometimes carved rocking horses when times were slack, and they might have been responsible for the development of this interesting construction.

Throughout the nineteenth century artists included rocking horses and pulltoys in portraits of little boys. Since young children of both sexes were usually dressed alike, horses identified boys just as dolls denoted girls.

The horse and rider, a recurrent image in folk art, appeared not only in pulltoys, weathervanes, and paintings but even in Pennsylvania German pottery. The "Schimmelreiter," a bold soldier on a white horse, was part of the folklore of the region. These ghostly riders on pale horses leading celestial armies referred to the Apocalypse described in Revelation: "And I saw heaven opened, and behold a white horse; and he that sat on him was called Faithful and True."[13]

In every town across eighteenth- and nineteenth-century America, riders tied their horses to hitching posts, which were usually simple wooden poles topped by cast-iron finials. The finials were made from molds cast from a wooden original. Finials in the shape of horses' heads were most popular, and often could be ordered from the same catalogue that featured weathervanes.

Horse with the Longest Hair in the World
Anonymous
Oil on canvas
18″ x 24″
1890s
New York State
Courtesy of the New York
State Historical Association,
Cooperstown

Rocking Horse
Anonymous
Painted wood
46″ x 23″
Early 19th century
Lancaster County, Pa.
Courtesy of Olde Hope
Antiques, New Hope, Pa.

An exceptional rocking
horse. The original 19th-
century coat of red paint still
remains. By the mid-19th
century, toy stores in cities
offered as many as five
different rocking horses in
various shapes and sizes.

Calligraphic Drawing of a
Woman on a Rearing Horse
"Professor Martin"
Ink on paper
36″ x 26″
1888
Hartford, Conn.
Courtesy of Hirschl &
Adler Folk, New York City
Photograph: Helga Photo
Studio

Rocking Horse
Anonymous
Wood with brass and
wood buttons
50″ x 25″
c. 1850
New England
Courtesy of Susan and
Sy Rapaport
Photograph:
Edward Shoffstall

Wealthy families often
commissioned skilled
cabinetmakers and
chairmakers to carve rocking
horses (by the mid-19th
century, the rocking horse
had become a favorite toy of
young boys).

Horse Cutter
Anonymous
Wood and metal
10″ length
19th century
New England
Courtesy of Kathy Schoemer,
North Salem, N.Y.

Sampler
Signed "Polly Shepard"
Cotton threads on home-
spun ground
15¾″ x 12¾″
1810
Connecticut
Courtesy of Kathy Schoemer,
North Salem, N.Y.
Photograph: Mike Levins

A horse tethered to an inn
sign was an unusual scene in
a sampler. (Note the age of
the artist.)

Homespun Horse
Anonymous
Homespun cotton, leather,
and wood (hooves)
6″ x 4½″
19th century
Courtesy of Kathy Schoemer,
North Salem, N.Y.
Photograph: Mike Levins

It is only recently that soft
toys have been regarded as
folk art. Like their cousins,
rag dolls, cloth toys that were
made from scrap material
entertain us with their
delightful ingenuity.

Horse Crock
Incised "West Troy Pottery"
Stoneware with cobalt
decoration
9″ height
1863–67
West Troy, N.Y.
Courtesy of Betty and Joel
Schatzberg, Riverside, Conn.

A horse of unusual
proportions decorates this
stoneware crock.

Pair of Bennington Lions
Fenton Works
Glazed stoneware
9⅜″ x 11″ x 5⅞″ each
1849
Bennington, Vt.
Courtesy of the Museum of
American Folk Art

Animals that were made as
small ornamental pieces were
not produced in great quan-
tity by the Bennington
Pottery. Each was based
on English prototypes in
Staffordshire and influenced
generations of folk sculptors
who adapted the forms and
the glazing.

Exotic Animals

ALTHOUGH THE HORSE was much admired in early America, it was a familiar animal and couldn't draw crowds except at the racetrack. However, the entire
populace of a town could not resist the special exhibitions or forerunners of the
circus. In 1788, Lancaster, Pennsylvania, enjoyed the opportunity of seeing one of
the first camels in America. *The New Unpartisan Lancaster Newspaper and Advertising
Directory* told of a camel being exhibited at the house of Thomas Edwards on
Queen Street for a week, with admission at elevenpence for adults (half price for
children).[14] Circuses, fairs, and special exhibitions all generated excitement that
ultimately was reflected in folk art. The following event in New York at the turn
of the nineteenth century is one such example:

> On Monday will be exhibited, The American Phenomena, just arrived from Phila-
> delphia, consisting of a fine little Bird, a beautiful flying Squirrel, a Rattlesnake and
> other Animals, living together in the same cage.[15]

At an exhibition or fair one might delight in the carousel or merry-go-round
that gaily turned with a satisfying array of exotic beasts. Descended from medieval

jousts and contests featuring knights astride horses in continual motion, the first carousels were made by wheelwrights and ship carvers. Known as "Flying Horses," early merry-go-rounds relied on actual horse power to pull the wooden animals around in a circle. A band sometimes played to enliven the proceedings. Early carousel animals were entirely hand-carved (in-the-round), free-standing sculptures. Interestingly, the outer sides were more elaborately carved than the inner sides. In keeping with the philosophy of not wasting time upon areas less exposed to the eye of the customer, the animals on the outside of the carousel were more ornate and larger than those on the inside. With the invention in 1879 of the pantograph, a machine that block-cut the rough form, the later carousels were only hand-finished and painted.

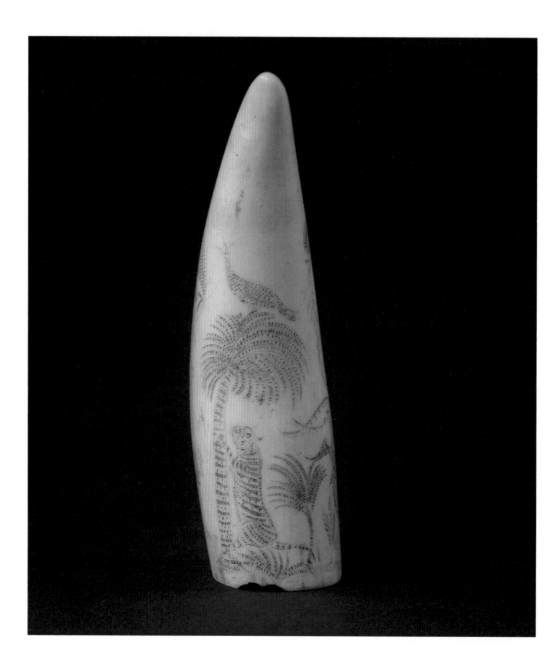

Tiger Scrimshaw
Unknown whaleman
Whale ivory (sperm
whale tooth)
6″ height
Dated 1847
New England, probably
Nantucket
Courtesy of
Barbara Johnson, Esq.
Photograph: Clem Fiori

Tiger Sculpture. Anonymous. Painted wood. 25″ height. 19th century.
Courtesy of Aarne Anton, New York City. Photograph: Steven Tucker

The artist was a virtuoso painter (note the undulating stripes enhancing the
tiger's beauty) as well as a talented carver.

Lion Sculpture. Anonymous! Ohio bluestone. 11″ x 9″.
c. 1860. Pennsylvania or Ohio. Courtesy of Steve Miller,
New York City

Reminiscent of the lions found in paintings by Edward Hicks,
this sculpture might have been based on engravings or trade
signs.

"Lion of the Day" Calligraphy
  George Nichols
  Ink on paper
  23⅓″ x 17¼″
  1850
  Wickford, R.I.
  Collection of William
  Glennon, Wiscasset, Maine
  Photograph courtesy of
  Maine Antiques Digest

The "Lion of the Day"
distributes broadsides bearing
the likeness of Jenny Lind
"drawn with a steel pen,"
honoring the Swedish
Nightingale's tour of Rhode
Island in 1850.

Lion Carving. Attributed to Knap Van Trump. Carved wood.
14″ x 7″. Late 19th century. Salem, Iowa. Courtesy of Main
Street Antiques & Art, West Branch, Iowa

Knap Van Trump, a blacksmith in Salem, Iowa, took up
whittling in his old age and gave away most of his carvings. He
may have been influenced by pictures of Egyptian sculpture
since his lion looks like those seen on Egyptian sarcophagi.

Carousel Horse. Stein and Goldstein. Carved and original polychromed wood. 58″ x 65″. c. 1915. Brooklyn, N.Y. Courtesy of Linda and Bruce Gottlieb

This front-row "stander" (other carousel horse styles include prancers and jumpers) is considered to be one of the finest carousel horses in America.

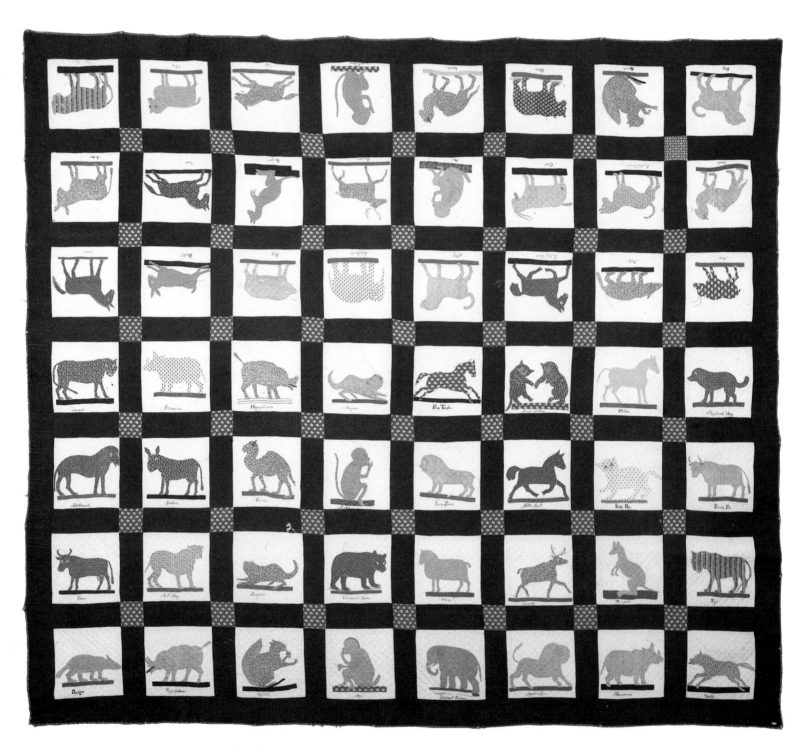

Lepp Family Album Quilt. Lepp family member. Cotton. 89″ x 100″.
Dated 1870. Pennsylvania. Collection of Robert and Katherine Booth.
Photograph courtesy of Suzanne Courcier and Robert W. Wilkins,
Austerlitz, N.Y.

A prized family heirloom with names and birth dates of Lepp family
members stitched in the borders of the quilt.

Chicken Carousel Figure
Herschell-Spillman
Company
Painted and carved wood
57″ x 43″
1902
North Tonowanda, N.Y.
Courtesy of Dr. and Mrs.
Sergio Prosperpi

The chicken, a second-row
carousel figure, last rode the
Fantasy Farm Carousel in
Middletown, Ohio. Years
later its paint was restored
by Charles Jakubowski
in Pennsylvania.

Lion Stoneware Crock
Incised "T. Harrington"
Stoneware
11″ height
1852–72
Incised "Lyons, N.Y."
Courtesy of Betty and Joel
Schatzberg, Riverside, Conn.

The lion's pose is unusual
on a stoneware crock. The
liberal use of expensive
cobalt suggests a special
gift or commission.

REVEREND JONATHAN FISHER (1768–1847)

Many Americans acquired their knowledge of animals that did not appear in everyday life from books or newspapers whose engravings were often derived from European prints and paintings. One of the first Americans to complete an extensive picture book of animals was Jonathan Fisher. In 1834, after working on 140 woodblocks of animals, reptiles, birds, and insects for over fourteen years, he published *Scripture Animals, or Natural History of the Living Creatures Named in the Bible, Written Especially for Youth* in Portland, Maine. Each woodcut had its own biblical reference, a "moral" observation, and a description of the species. He described a rooster as "A domestic fowl, often called the dung-hill Cock. It is not mentioned in the old Testament, but noticed several times in the new. . . ."[16] Some of his sketches were his own but many were copied from illustrations in books, among them the English engravings by Thomas Bewick. Alice Winchester, whose book on Fisher is a classic in the field of folk art studies, points out that "To a degree Fisher was typical of many American amateurs who produced pictures in great quantities and diverse mediums. . . . He was self-taught, he prepared his own materials and made his own tools, and his very lack of training and sophistication helped to give his work individuality."[7]

Fisher sought to broaden the education of those who read *Scripture Animals*. By labeling the animals in Hebrew and Greek (some also in French and Latin), he expressed his wish in the foreword to "raise a desire in the bosoms of some young persons of natural genius to seek an education." Probably his readers were more impressed by his vivid descriptions and drawings of various animals, including fieldmice who invaded the Maine and Massachusetts countryside in 1809 and the fox who spit out thirteen of them at a time. To counteract such irreverent humor, Fisher ended his delightful book with a tombstone inscribed with skull and bones and a Latin motto to the effect that "The sun sets; the shadows gather."

In addition to his books, Jonathan Fisher created portraits, landscapes, and still-life paintings while also attending his flock as the respected village parson of Blue-hill, Maine.

Elephant and Deer
Jonathan Fisher (1768–1847)
Woodcuts
Dimensions unavailable
1834
Blue Hill, Maine
Courtesy of the Jonathan Fisher Memorial Museum, Blue Hill, Maine

Woodcuts illustrated in *Scripture Animals* (1834).

Animal Hooked Rugs in
Early New England

THE HARSH WINTERS and isolation faced by settlers in Maine inspired a variety of arts, including the popular craft of rug hooking. The history of hooked rugs in America has its antecedents in small rugs for the hearthside or the bedchamber, but the answers to questions of where and when these rugs were first made remain somewhat of a mystery. It is thought that the technique developed in Canada and northern New England. These regions harbored maritime settlements, and there is speculation that rug hooks evolved from the marlinespike that sailors used in knotting mats.

Women throughout New England took up hooking as a pastime and as a means of inexpensively decorating their homes. Often they improvised from the material at hand. Designs were drawn with the burnt end of a stick or a piece of charcoal.

Tiger Hooked Rug
Anonymous
Wool on burlap
40″ x 23″
c. 1900
Courtesy of Patty Gagarin,
Fairfield, Conn.
Photograph: Luigi Pelletieri

When rugmakers wanted to reproduce circular shapes, they traced outlines of kitchen cups and pots. Dyes were usually vegetal concoctions made from recipes handed down in families. During westward journeys women used worn-out wagon covers as rug backings.

Hooked rugs generally fall into three categories: geometric, floral, and pictorial. Landscapes, seascapes, patriotic and religious scenes, homilies, tales from family histories, portraits, and historical events have all been hooked into pictorial rugs. Many rugs were inspired by the familiar animals around the house and barnyard, or were copied from books, rural newspapers, and ladies' magazines. The most interesting examples were often drawn from memory. Women took a free hand with their animals, feeling little need to follow the rules of proportion or perspective.

The stenciled patterns produced by Edward Frost in the 1860s introduced many women to the art of rug hooking. Frost, a Yankee peddler from Biddeford, Maine, tried his hand at a hooked rug his wife was making and decided he could design a more realistic rug using tin stencils. By 1876 he developed over 750 zinc stencils enabling him to print more than 180 designs. Women could order his patterns from large mail-order firms such as Montgomery Ward and Sears, Roebuck. Animal designs, including dogs, tigers, lions, and cats, were among the most popular motifs. The Montgomery Ward catalogue of 1887 included Frost's single most successful pattern, a spaniel, advertising it as "a large, intelligent dog." While stencils have been blamed for inhibiting the creative process, they often were used merely as taking-off points. Women added or subtracted figures, filled in the backgrounds with their own designs, and changed color combinations, thus keeping alive the tradition of creating an individualized art.

Domestic Zoo Hooked Rug
Magdalina Briner
Wool rag on burlap
75½" x 24"
1870
Pennsylvania
Courtesy of
Barbara Johnson, Esq.

Most hooked rugs are lacking in provenance. The "Domestic Zoo" is unusual in its documentation.

Baby and Dog Hooked Rug
Anonymous
Wool on burlap
41″ x 31″
Late 19th century
Courtesy of Patty Gagarin,
Fairfield, Conn.
Photograph: Luigi Pelletieri

Farm Scene Hooked Rug
Anonymous
Wool on burlap
60″ x 48″
c. 1900
New England
Courtesy of Patty Gagarin,
Fairfield, Conn.
Photograph: Luigi Pelletieri

This scene reflects the
pride of the rug hooker in
her livestock, farmhouse,
and barn.

Cat Hooked Rug
Anonymous
Wool on burlap
45″ x 28″
c. 1920
Courtesy of Elliott
and Grace Snyder,
South Egremont, Mass.

A study in contrasts—a very
folky cat against a geometric
backdrop that could pass as a
modern painting.

Cat Family Rug
Anonymous
Cotton and wool on burlap
42″ x 34″
19th century
Pennsylvania
Courtesy of Pam Martine,
Greenwich, Conn.
Photograph: Mike Levins

The maker has filled her rug
with a family of cats.

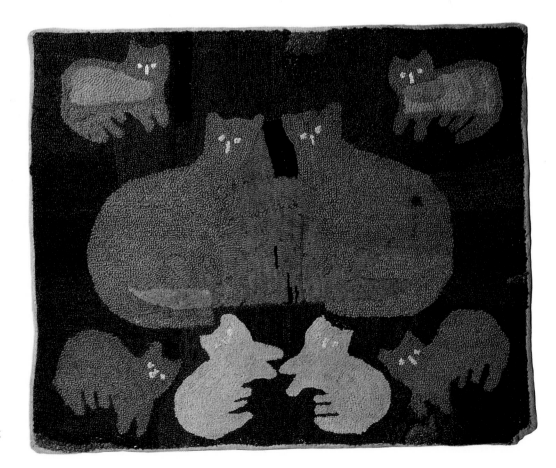

Dog Rug
Anonymous
Cotton and wool on burlap
28″ x 19″
c. 1920
Maine
Courtesy of Pam Martine,
Greenwich, Conn.
Photograph: Mike Levins

Many of the finest hooked
rugs come from Maine—
made during the long, harsh
winters. Often, the family
dog was chosen as a subject.

Turkey Hooked Rug
Anonymous
Wool on burlap
21½″ x 37″
1910
Maine
Courtesy of Patty Gagarin,
Fairfield, Conn.
Photograph: Luigi Pelletieri

Woman Feeding Brood of Chickens. Hooked Rug.
Anonymous. Wool on burlap. 44½″ x 17½″. c. 1900. Courtesy
of Kathy Schoemer, North Salem, N.Y. Photograph: Mike
Levins

In designing pictorial hooked rugs, many women chose subjects
from their everyday life. The woman who hooked this rug
probably had a brood of chickens she fed each day and for
whom she felt affection.

Waldoboro-Type Duck Rug
Anonymous
Wool on burlap
39″ x 21¾″
Late 19th century
Courtesy of Tony and
Marie Shank
Photograph: Ted Whisnant

The art of raised-pile rugs
originated in Waldoboro,
Maine, in the 19th century,
and has been used by rug
hookers in many areas of the
country to achieve special,
sculptural effects.

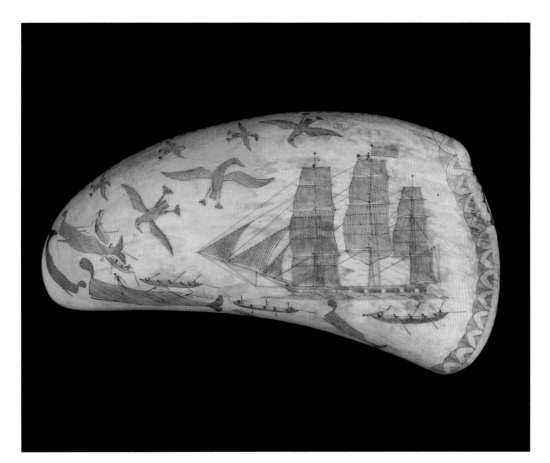

Scrimshaw

THE FISHING INDUSTRIES along the coast of Maine and throughout New England also saw the rise of such maritime arts as scrimshaw and figurehead carving. To reduce the tedium of long sea voyages, sailors painstakingly carved scrimshaw whimseys from the teeth and bones of the whale, often depicting the whale as well as other fish and seabirds encountered on their journeys. Sailors also chose as subjects animals that held special meaning to them—a favorite pet from home, a creature once seen at a fair, or an animal thought to be a talisman.

In addition to cutting out the tooth from the whale's lower jaw, many steps were involved in the process before a whaleman could incise the design with a knife or needle. Soaking, drying, filing, smoothing, and polishing were part of the process of scrimshaw. When the artist settled on his design, he often chose animal subjects from the Bible, such as the snake from the Garden of Eden, the whale from Noah's Ark, or the lion from Daniel in the Lion's Den.

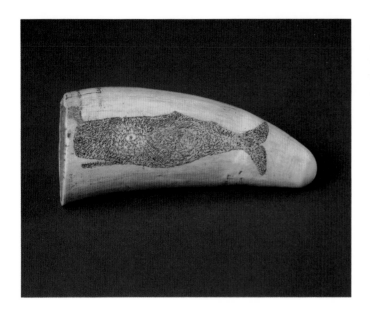

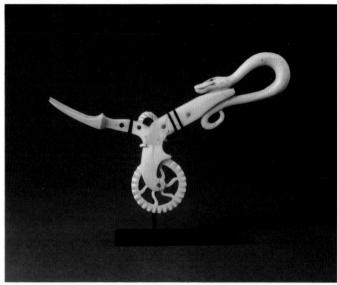

ABOVE LEFT:
Whale Scrimshaw
Anonymous whaleman
Whale ivory (sperm
whale tooth)
5⅝″ length
c. 1820
New Bedford, Mass.
Courtesy of
Barbara Johnson, Esq.
Photograph: Clem Fiori

This was etched by pinprick
scrimshaw, a laborious,
difficult technique.

ABOVE RIGHT:
Snake Pie Crimper
Unknown whaleman
Whale ivory and coin
silver with baleen inlays
and fastenings
6″ x 4″
c. 1850
New Bedford, Mass.
Courtesy of
Barbara Johnson, Esq.
Photograph: Clem Fiori

Pictures drawn in sailors' journals depicting scenes from the whaler's life also found their way into scrimshaw. Other sailors relied on whatever popular publications were available for scrimshaw designs. Using a pinprick technique to copy the drawings, animal scrimshaw was taken directly from engravings in magazines and newspapers. The sailor positioned the illustration over the tooth in order to push a small pin through the outlines of the design into the tooth itself. He then connected the dots to form a continuous line before filling in the design with black ink.[18]

Sailors produced an array of decorative objects for the home. For the kitchen alone whalemen carved pie crimpers, rolling pins, apple corers, cookie cutters, flatware, and many types of cutlery. Perhaps fond memories of home cooking inspired this output, as sailors labored over the jagging wheel, also known as a pie crimper. Many sailors chose animal motifs, fashioning handles in the shapes of such animals as snakes, horses, or fish. Others incised pictures of animals into the handles themselves or carved animal heads as tops of handles. Despite their practicality, these varied utensils were notable for their sculptural qualities.

Sailors carved corset stays for wives and sweethearts, frequently choosing to decorate them with animal motifs. Fish and birds appear with regularity, especially the whale and the eagle. Women also coveted the engraved whale's tooth as a trophy or talisman. The dimensions and shape of the tooth provided ample space for intricate designs featuring seascapes, landscapes, and a variety of scenes and "stories" related to the capture of the whale. Many of these whale teeth are now regarded as masterpieces of scrimshaw art.

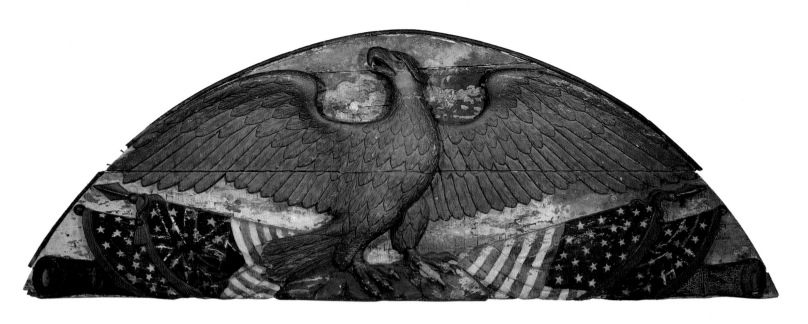

Ship Figureheads

FIGUREHEAD CARVING played an integral role in the fishing and shipbuilding industries. Figureheads not only identified ships but were thought to bring good luck—a scarce commodity on the perilous voyages in rough and often uncharted seas. Usually carved with chisels out of soft pine instead of the hardwoods favored in Europe, American figureheads were often polychromed for protection and decoration. Following English custom, the earliest figureheads on ships sailing from American ports were regal British lions. In 1689, a Boston carver's bill included a notation for a "lyon" for the sloop *Speedwell,* and in 1700 a ship, the *Pennsylvania Merchant,* was identified in a letter by its figurehead of a "Tafferil Lyon."[19]

By the middle of the eighteenth century vessels began appearing with horses and seahorses as figureheads. One wreck of a brig was reported in 1756 by the Boston *Gazette* as wearing a "Horse head," while the following year a wrecked schooner was described as carrying a "sea Horse head."[20] After the American Revolution the eagle replaced the lion in popularity. Other types of birds were also frequently depicted—such as the robin that adorned the ship *Robin.* The famous ship carver John Bellamy of Kittery, Maine, known for his splendid eagles, also created an unusual cat head for the end of the boom at the bow of a ship. It was used as a der-

Paddle Wheel Cover
Anonymous
Carved and painted wood
9′ x 3′
Mid-19th century
Great Lakes area
Courtesy of Wayne Pratt,
Marlborough, Mass.

The Naval Museum in Washington, D.C., believes this sternboard came from a warship.

rick to raise the anchor. Sailors grew attached to the figureheads of their ships, and often thought of them superstitiously as the guarantors of a safe voyage.

The Bear of Oakland, carved by William A. Robertson, was one animal figurehead that lived up to its reputation. Robertson, who sailed with the ship on the second Byrd expedition, carved the bear in the 1870s. After the United States acquired the ship in 1884, the *Oakland* and her bear figurehead guarded patrol boats for forty years, until she broke up in a storm off the coast of Cape Sable. Few figureheads achieved such longevity, leaving only a handful of these skillfully executed animal carvings to be admired today.

"Button" Fish
Anonymous
Painted wood, shells, buttons, metal, and nails
21¼" x 6"
1930s
Michigan
Courtesy of
Barbara Johnson, Esq.
Photograph: Clem Fiori

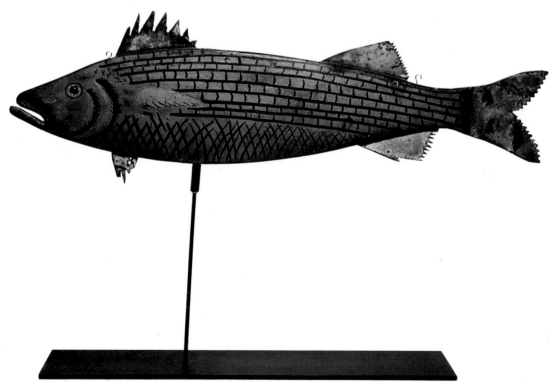

Fish Weathervane
Anonymous
Carved and painted gilded wood with copper fins and glass eyes
33½" x 14"
c. 1840s
Collection of Robert and Katherine Booth
Photograph courtesy of David A. Schorsch, New York City

This skillfully painted fish was created as a weathervane and was used at a later time as a trade sign (perhaps outside a fish market).

Fishing Industries in New England

THE FISH was the source of artistic inspiration for New England carvers. Many worked anonymously, but a few are still remembered today. Around 1760, John Welch carved a huge codfish in honor of the fishing industries of Massachusetts. After all, the codfish not only fed the settlers but was an important commodity exported to Europe. It could even be argued that the bulk of the shipbuilding industry was based on the export of dried codfish. Welch's sculpture was proudly hung in the Boston State House where it was dedicated as a "memorial to the importance of the cod fishery to the welfare of the commonwealth." Throughout the years Welch's codfish retained its place of honor and can still be seen today. As late as the 1880s a historian exclaimed: "Let me be clear, neither Pilgrims nor Puritans were its pioneers; neither the axe, the plough, nor the hoe led it to these shores; neither the devices of the chartered companies nor the commands of royalty. It was the discovery of the winter fishery on its shores that led New England to civilization."[21]

Years later, another Massachusetts painter and carver, J. O. J. Frost, sought to capture the bygone days of seafaring America with paintings of Marblehead harbor, ship models, and fish sculptures. He is best known for his fish carvings on which he painted nostalgic scenes of Marblehead.

To Frost and many other New Englanders the fish meant much more than a patriotic symbol—it reminded them of adventure on the high seas.

Painted Fish
J. O. J. Frost (1852–1928)
Painted wood
28″ x 11″
c. 1919–28
Marblehead, Mass.
Courtesy of the Marblehead Historical Society
Photograph: Jack Hunt

J. O. J. Frost, a self-taught artist who began to paint scenes of Marblehead after the death of his wife, provided a valuable record of the history of the town. He was especially interested in the fish and seabirds that graced the harbor.

Moravian Fish Bottle
Attributed to the shop of
Rudolph Christ
Press-molded, lead-glazed
earthenware
5″ x 2½″
c. 1802–20
North Carolina
Courtesy of the Museum of
Early Southern Decorative
Arts, Winston-Salem, N.C.

A rare fish bottle served as a
flask for liquor.

Crossed Fishes
Stoneware Crock
Incised "H. M. Whitman/
Havana N.Y."
Stoneware
1 gallon size, 7″ height
1860–62
Courtesy of Betty and Joel
Schatzberg, Riverside, Conn.

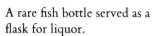

Ax Holder
Anonymous
Wrought iron
6″ x 4″
19th century
Lancaster County, Pa.
Courtesy of Sidney Gecker,
New York City

An ax holder that was carried
aboard the Conestoga wagon
that crossed the plains.

Salmon Weathervane
Anonymous
Painted metal silhouette
39″ length
c. 1900
Made for the Seufert
Cannery, The Dalles, Ore.
Courtesy of the Oregon
Historical Society

This salmon vane was
commissioned by the Seufert
Cannery and could be seen
from many parts of town.

Decoys

ALONG THE New England coastal regions decoys have been used for centuries. Archeologists found a cache of duck decoys dating from A.D. 1000 while excavating Indian relics from a Nevada cave in 1924. In 1687 a traveler to the New World wrote home telling how the Indians lured fowl with "the skins of Geese, Bustards, and Ducks, dry'd and stuff'd with Hay."²² The Indians fashioned their decoys out of woven bulrushes, twisting them into ducklike shapes. Decoys have been discovered with heads made from skeletons of real birds. Painted surfaces or skin and feather coverings created a realistic effect. The settlers were quick to copy this useful invention, adding some improvements of their own. Gradually hunters began carving more lifelike decoys, using more sophisticated tools and materials than those available to the coastal tribes.

Decoys represent one of the few indigenous American crafts, as the making of decoys was not dependent on European traditions. Its origins were rooted in the

Eider Duck Decoys
Anonymous
Polychromed wood
Left: 18½″ x 9½″
Right: 17¾″ x 8¼″
19th century
Maine
Courtesy of
Barbara Johnson, Esq.
Photograph: Clem Fiori

New World. The abundant supply of migrating birds that dotted American skies provided families with food even when the harvest failed or animals were scarce. Men in America, unlike their counterparts living under the system of feudalism in Europe, could hunt where they wished using decoys based on Indian prototypes.

In the early nineteenth century hunters favored heavy, low-floating wooden birds known as "rocking horses." Carvers tried to make decoys that handled well in the water and lured birds with reliability. In order to achieve more naturalistic decoys, men began carving with an eye for detail and refinement. Feather carving, for example, not only provided detail but also cut down the reflection of light that scared off potential prey. After the last feather was carved, hunters would seal the decoy with a protective undercoat of paint and apply a topcoat to identify the species. Painting varied widely, from precise patterns to more stylized and impressionistic work. Painters individualized their decoys by brushwork, graining combs, speckling, and many other techniques. Men who never considered themselves artists spent hours trying to achieve the desired painterly effect. Occasionally they would carve or brand their initials on the bottom of the finished product, usually as a mark of ownership rather than an artistic flourish. Hunters who had not made their own decoys would sometimes scratch their initials into their purchases to prevent loss or theft.

By the middle of the nineteenth century the growing demand for wild fowl ushered in the golden era of the decoy. So many decoys were made that every known species of shorebirds, ducks, gulls, swans, and geese was represented in decoy form. Many hunters carved their own decoys, while others relied on a newly developed cottage industry of skilled carvers who made decoys for sale. The men who carved decoys were an independent lot who took great pride in their work. While trying to faithfully copy a live bird, they still stamped each decoy with their

Canadian Geese Andirons
Anonymous
Cast iron
15″ x 28″ each
Late 19th century
Courtesy of Hirschl & Adler Folk, New York City

Andirons in the shape of ducks and geese were very popular with those who hunted, and were used in lodges and country homes.

personal style. Regional differences abound, with different areas producing decoys of the species most sought after by local hunters. Along the Atlantic coastline from Maine to the Carolinas decoys portrayed the eider, black, canvasback, and pintail ducks, along with the Canadian goose and a variety of shorebirds.[23]

The decoys that transcended their original function to become objects of art are those that evoke the life of the bird. The best decoy makers were perceptive observers. They knew the way a duck tucked his head under his wing, and therefore they could re-create his stance with a convincing naturalism. Artists who succeeded in portraying the essence of wild fowl were not only great carvers but also talented painters who could convey the lightness of a feather. A decoy tradition evolved based on aesthetics of abstract beauty as well as refined detail.

By the 1920s shorter hunting seasons and declining migrations gradually signaled an end to the age of the decoy. When many of the master carvers died, they were not replaced by new craftsmen; the decoy became a lost art.

Eiders on an Ice Flow
Edward Akin
Oil on board
26″ x 16″
1870
Dartmouth, Mass.
Courtesy of
Barbara Johnson, Esq.
Photograph: Clem Fiori

A scene of Point Barrow in the Arctic.

Duck Rocking Horse
Anonymous
Wood with glass eyes
33″ x 19″
Late 19th century
Virginia
Courtesy of
Mr. and Mrs. James Clokey
Photograph:
Edward Shoffstall

This rare "rocking duck" was carved by a decoy maker, but was never intended to be a decoy (its neck is too long!).

Sickle-Billed Curlew
Mason Factory
Wood, metal, and glass
7⅞″ x 17⅜″ x 4½″
1925
Detroit, Mich.
Courtesy of the Museum of American Folk Art

The curlew is well represented in decoy form as it is the largest and most distinguished of the shorebirds.

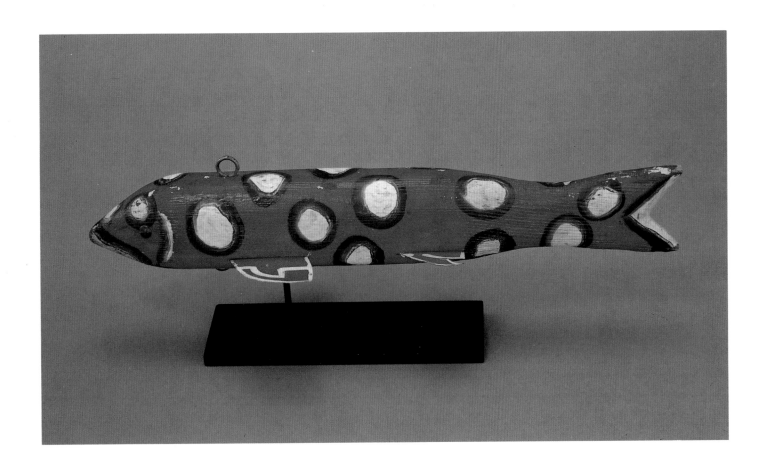

Fish Decoys

ORIGINALLY USED by Eskimos and midwestern Indians, fishing decoys attracted their prey. By chopping holes in the ice and dropping hand-carved decoys into the frigid waters of the Great Lakes, they lured the fish to their spears. During the nineteenth century American fishermen carved and painted decoys in sizes varying from a few inches to a few feet. Although today's fisherman usually prefers the mass-produced plastic decoys, there are fishing enthusiasts who still carve and paint their own decoys. Makers frequently carve their decoys out of soft pine and paint them with bright, often iridescent colors. When glitter, rhinestones, bits of mirror, and other shiny materials are added, the results can be imaginative as well as eye-catching. The use of found and everyday materials such as coffee cans and thumbtacks adds to the charm of these fish whimseys. Since decoys must withstand the rigors of being underwater for long periods of time, very few nineteenth-century examples survive. Most of the fishing decoys collected today as folk art date from the early twentieth century.

"Watermelon" Fish
Anonymous
Painted wood and tin
12¾" x 4¼"
1940s
Michigan
Courtesy of
Barbara Johnson, Esq.
Photograph: Clem Fiori

This decoy must have easily attracted fish in the icy waters off of Michigan.

Tortoise Ice-Fishing Decoys. Gray Eagle. Polychromed wood.
8″ x 3¾″ each. 20th century. Midwest. Courtesy of Barbara
Johnson, Esq. Photograph: Clem Fiori

Gray Eagle, a Native American, carved and painted these
accurate renditions of a box tortoise and a snapping tortoise;
they were to be used as ice-fishing decoys.

Turtle Ice-Fishing Decoy
Anonymous
Wood with studded nails
6¼″ x 2½″
1910
Courtesy of
Barbara Johnson, Esq.
Photograph: Clem Fiori

As a form, the turtle ice-
fishing decoy is rare. By
studding the turtle's "shell"
with nails, the decoy was
both decorative and practical
—the studs reflected the light
and attracted fish.

BELOW RIGHT:
"Submarine" Fish Decoy
Anonymous
Polychromed wood, metal,
and pieces of inlaid mirror
13¾″ x 4¾″
1940s
Michigan
Courtesy of
Barbara Johnson, Esq.
Photograph: Clem Fiori

The maker of this ice-fishing
decoy carefully planned his
design, using bits of inlaid
mirror for the portholes.
Glittery materials such as
rhinestones and colored glass
were quite often used as lures
and decoration.

Blue Gill Ice-Fishing Decoy
Anonymous
Wood and tin
10″ x 6″
c. 1930s–40s
Minnesota
Courtesy of Main Street
Antiques & Art,
West Branch, Iowa

This fish decoy is
unusual because of its
sponge decoration.

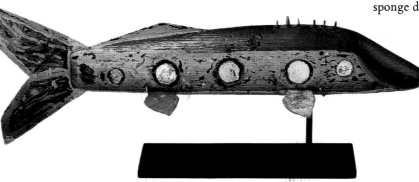

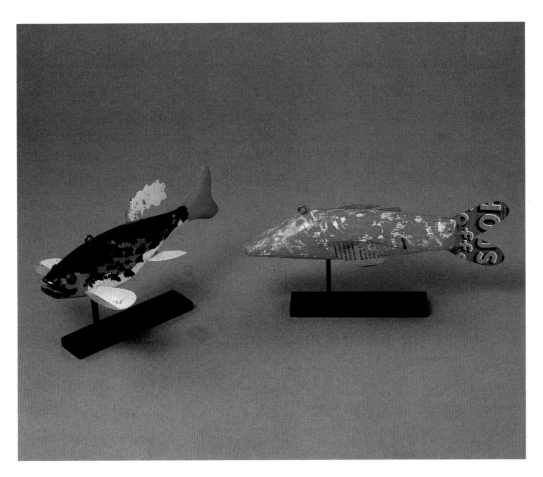

Ice-Fishing Decoys
Left: Scalloped Fin Decoy
Anonymous
Polychromed wood
and metal
7″ x 4″
c. 1920s–30s
Wisconsin
Right: "Maxwell House"
Fish Decoy
Anonymous
Polychromed wood
and metal
7¾″ x 3″
c. 1940s
Minnesota
Courtesy of
Barbara Johnson, Esq.
Photograph: Clem Fiori

Folk artists have always
converted "found" materials
into art, as the Maxwell
House Coffee tin fish on the
right illustrates.

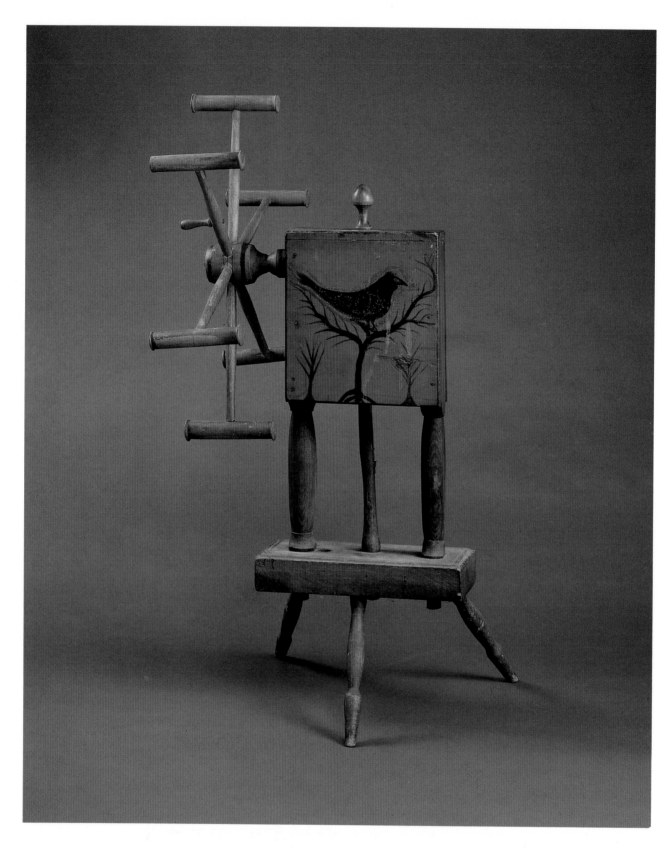

Bird-Decorated Yarnwinder. Anonymous. Painted wood. Dimensions
unavailable. Mid-19th century. New England. Courtesy of Olde Hope
Antiques, New Hope, Pa.

A rare example of a decorated handmade yarnwinder.

The Pennsylvania Germans

FURTHER SOUTH among the Pennsylvania Germans the depiction of animals
in frakturs and in ordinary household furnishings developed from a European heritage of illuminated manuscripts. The lion and the unicorn, borrowed from the
English coat of arms, appear on dower chests, and a variety of beasts can be seen in
the alphabets of almanacs.[24] During the richest period of Pennsylvania German art
(1750–1850) animals were an integral part of the scene. The ornamental drawings
and calligraphy of frakturs are enlivened by an array of decorative animals and
birds. Folk artists immortalized the birds they saw every day, including the distelfink, the ebullient bluebird, and even the parrot—once a frequent visitor emigrating from the Carolinas. The distelfink has often been connected to Pennsylvania
German folk art. One authority goes so far as to state that "Just as the eagle came
to symbolize America . . . so has the distelfink come to symbolize . . . the Pennsylvania Dutch."[25]

Birds almost always appeared on Pennsylvania German show towels—the
embroidered towels placed over the regular roller towels. Some young girls traced

Reward of Merits
Anonymous
Watercolor and ink on paper
Left: 4½″ x 3¾″
Right: 5″ x 4¼″
Mid-19th century
Pennsylvania
Courtesy of Sidney Gecker,
New York City

Reward-of-merit cards or
small paintings were awarded
to students for good behavior
and academic achievement.
Flowers and birds, popular
motifs, were created using
quills, pens, compasses, and
watercolors, reflecting the
fine skills of schoolmasters,
many of whom produced
some of the best Pennsylvania
German art.

their designs from the ubiquitous printed birth certificates, which featured two angels and two pairs of large birds, or they copied birds from pattern books that were handed down in the family. On some of the prettiest towels the birds are peacocks, a favorite Pennsylvania German motif. The peacock, at first glance a rather flamboyant figure for the prim Pennsylvania maiden, is foremost a biblical symbol. In the Old Testament the peacock allowed the serpent to enter the Garden of Eden and in the New Testament it is a symbol of the Resurrection. Barnyard fowl peacocks were so common in Pennsylvania that "their presence gave rise to a well-known weather adage: when the peafowl cries, there will be rain."[26]

Peacocks were embroidered on show towels and also were the subject for woven coverlets, spatterware china, intaglio-carved cake molds, cookie cutters, toys, reverse-painting mirrors, toleware, and wood carvings. An art whose fragile product has all but disappeared was the brightly colored stuffed peacock toys with cut-paper crests and fantails. Made by Pennsylvania German housewives "just for fancy" from odd scraps of material and paper, they were mounted on polychromed spools.[27] While artists depicting peacocks in frakturs, samplers, and show towels were limited by size requirements, the toleware artists of the Victorian period could indulge in peacocks with magnificent tail plumage.

Scherenschnitte
Anonymous
Paper on velvet
11″ height x 13″ length
Dated 1851
Probably Pennsylvania
Courtesy of Lillian and
Jerry Grossman
Photograph:
Edward Shoffstall

Traditionally made by young women, the art of scherenschnitt (paper cutouts) had its roots in a popular art form, the silhouette. It was favored by the German settlers in Pennsylvania, West Virginia, and North Carolina.

Miniature Hanging
Wall Cupboard
Anonymous
Painted wood
16″ x 8″ x 4″
Late 19th century
Mahantongo Valley, Pa.
Courtesy of Maureen and
David Haska

Deer frequently decorated Pennsylvania German furniture. Another cupboard made by the same carver is in the Metropolitan Museum of Art in New York City.

Sampler
Anonymous
Silk and watercolor on linen
20″ x 22″
c. 1820
Delaware Valley
Courtesy of Sheila and
Edwin Rideout

Snake Trivet
Anonymous
Wrought iron
10½″ length
18th century
Pennsylvania
Courtesy of Sidney and
Sandra Gecker

Eagle Door Latch
Anonymous
Wrought iron
18″ height
18th century
Lancaster County, Pa.
Photograph courtesy of
Sidney Gecker,
New York City

A decorative, functional form
with typical Pennsylvania
motifs—the tulip and the
eagle.

Dove Printing Block. Anonymous. Carved wood. 3¼″ x 2⅝″. 19th century.
Pennsylvania. Courtesy of the Museum of American Folk Art

Doves or lovebirds, symbolizing the human spirit or conveying sentiments
of the heart, often appear in Pennsylvania German folk art.

Wooden Box
Inscribed "Presented to
John Hunt
on his 8th Birthday
November 22 1855"
Painted pine
12″ x 5″
Courtesy of Lillian and
Jerry Grossman
Photograph:
Edward Shoffstall

Obviously a labor of love,
this carefully painted box
with its parade of animals
and alphabet letters was
meant to hold a collection of
young John Hunt's treasures.

Rabbit Family
Signed "Shilling"
Oil on canvas
12″ x 9″
19th century
Shillington, Pa.
Courtesy of Dr. and Mrs.
Sergio Prosperpi

It is believed this painting
was the work of C. Schilling,
from the family who
founded Shillington,
Pennsylvania.

Dove Knife Box
Anonymous
Walnut
14″ x 6″
c. 1830
Pennsylvania
Photograph courtesy of
Sidney Gecker,
New York City

The Pennsylvania Germans
saw the dove as a symbol of
conjugal bliss. This intricately carved knife box was
probably a wedding present.

Redware Bird Bank
Incised on bottom of bank:
"H. J. Robinson May 14,
1889"
Redware with lead glaze
6″ height
Pennsylvania
Courtesy of Tony and
Marie Shank
Photograph: Ted Whisnant

A number of redware bird
banks have been found,
indicating their popularity.
The inscription on the
bottom of the piece suggests
that it might have been a gift.

Soft Sculpture Animals
Anonymous
Cloth stuffed with cotton
and fabric remnants
3″–12″ height
1880s–1930s
Carlisle, Pa.
Courtesy of Kate Manko

These creatures from Noah's
Ark are part of a group made
by one woman over a period
of fifty years. Many women,
including those from the old
Amish sect, sewed animal
forms, sometimes taking their
inspiration from small hand-
carved animals.

Redware Peacock
William Gleaves
Redware with lead glaze
7½″ x 5½″
c. 1900
Montgomery County, Pa.
Courtesy of Tony and
Marie Shank
Photograph: Ted Whisnant

The spreading fantail feathers
of the peacock are difficult to
achieve in pottery. Note how
thin the feathers appear.

Covered Cake Dish with Bird Finial
Incised under lid: "A. E. Clark—Made by John M. Stout, Ripley, Illinois"
Albany-type slip-glazed stoneware
9½" height x 10" depth
c. 1850–75
Courtesy of Tony and Marie Shank
Photograph: Ted Whisnant

Animal Pottery

IN SPITE OF a limited number of decorative techniques, early American potters produced a variety of figurative designs. From New England to remote western outposts, birds, fish, and beasts graced jugs, crocks, plates, and pots of every description. Whether sculptural reliefs, finials, or painted decoration, animal motifs represented a spontaneous form of expression. Commercial potteries recognized the appeal of animal designs and incorporated them in many types of wares. By 1800 the marketplace was saturated with stoneware and earthenware motifs of animals, winged insects, fish, and birds. A number of animals were incised or molded, but most were painted with cobalt.

Gradually children's toys in the forms of bird whistles and animal coin banks were included as stock items in stores or available by special order. Very few examples survived as so many were broken in play.

Wild Boar Stoneware Crock
Attributed to MacQuoid
Pottery
Decorated stoneware
7½″ height
19th century
New York City
Courtesy of
Betty and Joel Schatzberg,
Riverside, Conn.

The wild boar is a rare motif.
The stoneware crock might
have been a commission or
an end-of-the-day piece to
please the artist.

Rooster Bank
Initialed "A.H."
Redware
6″ height
Mid-19th century
Ohio
Courtesy of Main Street
Antiques & Art, West
Branch, Iowa

Banks in the shape of animals
were made by a number of
American potteries—favorite
subjects included pigs,
chickens, and birds. Potters
often outdid themselves in
applying unusual and beautiful glazes to these pieces.

Trivet Pot with Bird-Chasing-Cricket Decoration. Chester Webster. Salt-glazed stoneware. 5″ height. Mid-19th century. Randolph County, N.C. Courtesy of Tony and Marie Shank. Photograph: Ted Whisnant

An "action portrait" in stoneware, this unusual trivet pot probably depicts the only bird-chasing cricket in stoneware.

Redware Bird Whistle. Anonymous. Redware. 4″ x 3″. c. 1840. New England. Courtesy of Kathy Schoemer, North Salem, N.Y. Photograph: Mike Levins

The beauty of this bird whistle lies in its form and unusual glazing with manganese highlights. The redware bird whistles were originally intended as toys and are now rare; the few that exist are highly prized as sculptures.

Pig Matchsafe
Kirkpatrick Brothers, Anna Pottery
Salt-glazed stoneware with incised cobalt lettering
6½″ x 1½″
Dated 1889
Anna, Ill.
Courtesy of Tony and Marie Shank
Photograph: Ted Whisnant

The inscription on the base reads: "What is a home without a mother" (also the title of a popular song written in 1854). The matchsafe was made for F. Rarsmeyor of Cairo, Illinois.

Stoneware Figural Pig Bottle. George Ohr. Stoneware with Albany slip glaze. 12″ x 4½″. Dated March 25, 1882. Biloxi, Miss. Courtesy of Tony and Marie Shank. Photograph: Ted Whisnant

George Ohr, the celebrated and eccentric potter from Mississippi, was twenty-five years old when he made this pig. The inscriptions on each side read: "Suck this hog's nose for gin" (back), and (front) "Mr. Murphy don't drink, but always keeps a little good old rye for his friends in this hogs's . . ."—a hand inscribed in the rear of the pig points to the opening in the rear. This is the earliest dated piece of George Ohr pottery.

Pie Plate
Anonymous
Slip-decorated redware
11½″ diameter
19th century
Matawan, N.J.
Private collection
Photograph courtesy of
Sidney Gecker,
New York City

While most utilitarian redware has vanished, slip- and sgraffito-decorated pottery has survived, since it was not used as everyday ware.

Lion Figure
Attributed to Solomon Bell
(d. 1882)
Earthenware with lead glaze
11″ x 6″ x 14½″
c. 1850
Strasburg, Va.
Courtesy of the Museum of
Early Southern Decorative
Arts, Winston-Salem, N.C.

One of four known lions
made by Solomon Bell for
his family. The lion figures
were used as doorstops.

Shenandoah Folk Pottery

POTTERS IN southern Pennsylvania and Virginia (the Shenandoah Valley), in addition to producing utilitarian ware, created a body of animal sculpture and pottery as commissions and gifts. These German immigrants and their sons were responsible for some of the most exciting animal pottery in nineteenth-century America. Many potteries were family-owned, so it is not surprising that animals "ran in families."

The Bell family pottery (active from 1824 to 1882) was founded by Peter Bell. His son, John, is best known for three major lion sculptures. By forcing clay through rough burlap, he achieved a "coleslaw" effect that became a trademark of his lions. Bell also favored Staffordshire-type spaniels and whippets that were popular with customers, who specially ordered them. His brother, Samuel Bell, made small animals, particularly dogs and cats; another brother, Solomon Bell, employed the lion as a motif for applied handles in his pottery, as well as for full-figured sculpture. The Bell pottery often featured an eagle in a spread-winged pose on mugs and vases. Glazed redware picture frames adorned with molded eagles,

Spaniel
Anonymous
Glazed redware
5″ height
c. 1840
Probably Virginia
Courtesy of Sidney Gecker,
New York City

Styled after Bennington
ware. The spaniel is a
Staffordshire derivative.

Seated Poodle
Anonymous
Glazed redware
10½″ height; 7½″ at base
c. 1860–80
Shenandoah Valley, Va.
Courtesy of Sidney Gecker,
New York City

An unusually large and rare
form to come out of a
Shenandoah pottery. It most
likely was a commissioned
gift. Note the tricolored
glazing.

sold by the pottery to be used for family portraits, were commercially successful, as were glazed and non-glazed sleeping lambs intended for children's grave markers. All of the animals produced by the Bell Pottery Works were notable for their beautiful mottled glazes and appealing expressions.

In Winchester, Virginia, from 1851 to 1889, Anthony Baecher worked in his own style, creating a body of animal pottery that includes a goat and a seated "coleslaw" bear holding a dog. Baecher also made sugar bowls accompanied by lids topped with feeding birds. Only a few of his works survive, so much has to be surmised about the extent of his production.

Whippet
John Bell (1800–1880)
Painted redware
11″ x 5½″
c. 1840–50
Waynesboro, Pa.
Courtesy of Sidney Gecker,
New York City

The only whippet by John
Bell, one of the most famous
Shenandoah potters, not
made on a base. It is also
unusual in that the whippet
is painted rather than glazed.

Covered Bowl with
Bird Finial
James Mackley
Redware with brown
slip glaze
5¾″ height
Dated 1869
Thurmont, Md.
Courtesy of Sidney Gecker,
New York City

The earliest known signed
and dated piece by
James Mackley, a famous
Maryland potter.

Seated Cat
Anonymous
Polychromed chalkware
15⅝″ x 8¾″ x 18⅛″
1860–1900
Pennsylvania
Courtesy of
David A. Schrosch,
New York City

Of monumental scale for
chalkware, only a few of
these pieces survive.

Pair of Poodles
Anonymous
Chalkware
4½″ height each
19th century
Pennsylvania
Courtesy of Sidney Gecker,
New York City

This pair of poodles was modeled after their more illustrious Staffordshire cousins. Pairs of animals were common in chalkware and were intended to sit on either side of a mantel clock.

Nineteenth-Century Chalkware

AKIN TO Shenandoah animals were the gaily colored chalkware sculptures found in shops and roadside stands dotting the Pennsylvania landscape. Often known as the poor man's Staffordshire, chalkware animal forms were modeled after creatures found on the farm or in neighboring fields—cats, dogs, rabbits, goats, sheep, squirrels, deer, and birds. For housewives wanting a knickknack or two, these inexpensive plaster-of-Paris ornaments were the answer.

Little information is available about the origins of chalkware—the name itself is a misnomer, but it probably was derived from the chalky characteristics of plaster-of-Paris. It is likely these folk sculptures descended from a European tradition that drew from the colorful Italian plaster Madonnas brought into the Rhineland countries. These religious figures eventually phased into the menagerie of household ornaments in faraway Pennsylvania.

The early chalkware figures were hollow—made from two or more part-earthenware molds that cast the quick-setting plaster. After the molds were unfastened and the cast removed, craftsmen smoothed the rough joining seams. Until this point the figures were all alike; it was in the painting (either by watercolors or oils) that fanciful colors applied with a small brush brought life to chalkware. Artists could work quickly without resorting to expensive equipment and glazes, thus keeping costs down. Although most chalkware decorated Pennsylvania German homes, occasional pieces wandered far afield. Indeed, chalkware did not escape the eye of nineteenth-century novelists, including Mark Twain, whose Huckleberry Finn saw some in a home near Hannibal, Missouri, and Harriet Beecher Stowe, who in *Uncle Tom's Cabin* refers to "some plaster images in resplendent colors on the mantel shelf" in an Ohio River tavern.[28]

Because chalkware during its day was never regarded as fine art, craftsmen felt free to borrow forms and decorative styles from a variety of sources. The ubiquitous roosters, hens, parrots, and eagles, for example, resemble the forms seen in redware. Spotted deer look remarkably like the Bennington Pottery deer, while sheep and dogs hark back to their Staffordshire cousins. After its initial popularity in the nineteenth century, chalkware was relegated to the attic, until the resurgence of folk art in the 1920s. Earl Robacker, one of the foremost scholars of the Pennsylvania Dutch, notes in *Touch of the Dutchland* (1965) that chalkware came as close to meeting a strict definition of "folk" art as did any American-made product: "Its forms were derived from everyday, familiar objects; its execution called for skill but not schooling; it satisfied a craving for color and beauty in an understood medium. Its evolutionary period was short; it seems to have achieved its peak in quality with almost, if not quite, its first production."[29]

Chalkware used to be sold at roadside stands and in five-and-ten-cent stores; today it is seen in prestigious private collections and museums throughout the country.

Four-Part Rooster Mold
Anonymous
Painted solid plaster
Largest mold: 8¼" x 6¾"
1860–1900
Probably Pennsylvania
Courtesy of the Museum of
American Folk Art

While chalkware was mass-produced in this kind of mold, no two figures were exactly alike. Individuality was bestowed by the artist, who painted the features according to his taste.

Swan
Anonymous
Chalkware
4¾'' x 4½''
1860–1900
Pennsylvania
Courtesy of the Museum of
American Folk Art

One of the more unusual
forms of chalkware.

Reclining Ewe and Lamb
Anonymous
Chalkware
6¼'' x 9''
1860–1900
Pennsylvania
Courtesy of the Museum of
American Folk Art

Did the artist just not finish
painting these figures, or did
he intend to color only the
faces? Note the ''chalkiness''
of the medium.

Cat Doorstop
Anonymous
Carved and painted pine
11″ length
c. 1850
Pennsylvania
Courtesy of Olde Hope
Antiques, New Hope, Pa.

Traces of olive paint and a
red scalloped collar reveal the
original 19th-century patina.

Wood Carving

WHITTLING SMALL ANIMALS was second nature to the Pennsylvania Germans and New England and midwestern farmers. It was regarded as a pastime that conveniently employed one's everyday tools such as the ax, chisel, and pocketknife. When one old-time wood carver was asked how to carve a horse, he responded: "Simple . . . just take a big block of wood and cut away everything that doesn't look like a horse."[30]

This matter-of-fact approach came naturally to the German immigrants, who were mostly farmers and craftsmen. Fathers needed little urging to carve dozens of animals for a Noah's Ark or the traditional Christmas Putz (a delightful nativity scene set around the Christmas tree). Squeak or bellows toys made out of papier-mâché attached to painted wooden bases were also popular. Usually representing birds and barnyard fowl, these toys were originally made in Germany, but some Pennsylvania Germans copied them. Men attached a wire to the body of the bird and connected it to a small spring whistle inside the base to produce a squeak. These tiny toys, usually around five inches high, were traditional Christmas gifts.

OPPOSITE PAGE:
Bird Tree
Steven Deady
Carved walnut
24½″ height
c. 1900
Galena, Ill.
Courtesy of the Artvest
Collection

Steven Deady, the shoemaker
who carved this tree, was a
French Canadian who
emigrated to Illinois.

Dove Rooftop Finial
Anonymous
Painted wood
13″ length
Early 20th century
Maine
Courtesy of Hirschl &
Adler Folk, New York City
Photograph: Steven Tucker

OPPOSITE PAGE: Etagère. Anonymous. Carved and painted wood. 8′ height. c. 1890s. Lancaster, Ohio. Courtesy of John Long. Photograph: Edward Shoffstall

The inscription on a plate on the left drawer reads: "Why are you sad?" The answer is found on the right side of the piece: "Someday I will wander back again." The carver mysteriously disappeared after completing this étagère.

Bird Cane with Ball. Anonymous. Painted wood. 36½″ height. c. 1880s.
Pennsylvania. Courtesy of Barbara Johnson, Esq. Photograph: Clem Fiori

This unusual cane has the characteristics of a whimsey.

Owl Decoy. Anonymous. Painted wood. 15½″ x 6″. c. 1920. Probably
Ohio. Courtesy of Fredric I. Thaler, Cornwall Bridge, Conn.

Made for a garden to scare away crows and other critters. Many owl decoys
were used to lure crows into target range, allowing farmers to protect their
cornfields.

Rooster Pulltoy
Anonymous
Composition and wood
5½" x 11"
19th century
Pennsylvania
Courtesy of Bernard and
Dean Levy, New York City

Pig Pulltoy
Anonymous
Carved wood, glass eyes, and
wire "corkscrew" tail
11¼" x 13¾"
Late 19th century
Courtesy of Tony and
Marie Shank
Photograph: Ted Whisnant

Carved wooden platform toys
were among the most popular
toys in the 19th century.
They were whittled and
painted by fathers, uncles,
and grandfathers, and
cherished by both girls
and boys.

Cow Butter Mold
Anonymous
Carved wood
3/4″ diameter
19th century
Courtesy of Lillian and
Jerry Grossman
Photograph:
Edward Shoffstall

Butter molds often display
cows standing underneath the
branch of a tree, in a grassy
field; occasionally, like this
one, the cows are carved with
full udders.

Oddfellows Plaque
Anonymous
Carved and painted wood
24″ square
c. 1915
Ohio
Courtesy of Allan Katz

This plaque, the lamb of
innocence, was made for an
Oddfellows meeting hall and
was very likely carved by one
of the group's members.

Crested Swans
John Scholl (1827–1916)
Carved and painted wood
88¼″ x 33″ x 30½″
c. 1910
Germania, Pa.
Courtesy of the Memorial
Art Gallery of the University
of Rochester

Using only a pocketknife,
John Scholl carved his
fanciful creations between
1907 and 1916. He favored
traditional Pennsylvania
designs embellished with
Victorian fretwork. After
emigrating from Germany to
the United States at the age
of twenty-six, he worked as a
carpenter until the latter part
of his life when he carved
forty sculptures.

Suffolk Lamb. Anonymous. Carved and painted wood. 20¼″ height. 19th century. Hirschl & Adler Folk, New York City

In this meticulously carved sculpture each tuft of wool is defined; the smooth rendering of the legs and head offers an interesting contrast to the textured body.

Swan Whimsey
Anonymous
Carved wood
8½″ x 2¾″
19th century
Courtesy of Lillian and
Jerry Grossman
Photograph:
Edward Shoffstall

Squirrel Gatepost
Anonymous
Carved oak
16″ height
Late 19th century
New England
Courtesy of Kenneth and
Ida Manko

Although the anonymous
New England carver whittled
this squirrel for a gatepost, he
also created an object of great
tenderness.

Eagle Sculpture
Wilhelm Schimmel
(1817–1890)
Carved and painted wood
20″ x 41″
1865–90
Cumberland County, Pa.
Courtesy of the Museum of
American Folk Art

WILHELM SCHIMMEL (1817–1890)
AND AARON MOUNTZ (1873–1949)

It is ironic that the most celebrated Pennsylvania German sculptor of animals was not an upstanding, hardworking family man like most of the Pennsylvania settlers, but, instead, an itinerant drunk whose ferocious temper made him an outcast among his neighbors. An obituary in the Carlisle, Pennsylvania, *Evening Sentinel* (August 7, 1890) reported:

> "Old Schimmel," the German who for many years tramped through this and adjoining counties making his headquarters in jails and almshouses, died at the almshouse on Sunday. His only occupation was carving heads of animals out of soft pine wood. These he would sell for a few pennies each. He was apparently a man of very surly disposition.[31]

It appears that Schimmel arrived in the Cumberland Valley shortly after the Civil War with his basket of hand-carved animals, which he tried to sell or barter for food or, more often, a pint of whiskey. It is said that by the time of his death every tavern in Carlisle boasted a Schimmel eagle. Although his small ornaments were used as mantel decorations, his large eagles perched atop tall poles graced a variety of gardens and schoolyards. However, in his lifetime Schimmel received little praise or encouragement. In competitions his rough-hewn animals made from soft pine lost out to carvings of black walnut testifying to Germanic precision. At one Cumberland Fair in the 1880s Schimmel fell into a rage when he failed to win a ribbon for his entry and heatedly cursed the judge.[32]

Schimmel's style was unique. Using leftover wood from barn-raisings and discarded railroad ties, he used his pocketknife to carve animals in a detailed yet impressionistic style. A prolific carver, it is estimated that Schimmel turned out at least five hundred roosters alone, ranging from two inches to twelve inches in height.[33] He is best known for his eagles, on which he labored to individualize each feather while at the same time creating an overall sawtooth pattern. His beaks were famous—bright red or yellow painted protuberances that seemed to belong on parrots rather than eagles. After applying gesso, Schimmel then liked to paint them. His larger birds required tremendous effort—the wings had to be created separately and then dovetailed to the body. Still, even with his larger eagles, the birds possess that magical quality of being poised for flight.

Despite his temper, a group of young boys often clustered around Schimmel, admiring his work while urging their pocketknives to work the same wonders out of blocks of wood. Among these boys was Aaron Mountz, also a German immigrant, who became a disciple of the crusty old man. Although Mountz was only seventeen when Schimmel died, he had learned his lessons well and became the only carver of Schimmel's "circle" to achieve fame. Although he always remained

Eagle Sculpture
Attributed to Aaron Mountz
(1873–1949)
Carved pine
8″ x 12″ x 5½″
Late 19th century
Cumberland Valley, Pa.
Hirschl & Adler Folk,
New York City

This sculpture is remarkable for its unique wings. Compared to the heaviness of the body, the wings appear ready to soar.

Poodle
Aaron Mountz (1873–1949)
Carved pine
5½″ x 7″
Late 19th century
Cumberland Valley, Pa.
Courtesy of Hirschl & Adler
Folk, New York City

Aaron Mountz's pieces are
distinguished from those
of his mentor, Wilhelm
Schimmel, by the laboriously
worked, even-patterned
carving.

in Schimmel's shadow (even though neighbors would exclaim, "As good as Schimmel!"), his animals merit distinction on their own.[34]

Inspired by the birds he saw near the creek by his house, Mountz sought to define his sculptures by meticulous patterns of crosshatching. Where Schimmel preferred a rough patina covered with paint, Mountz labored to produce a smooth, unpainted finish. His meticulousness might have been responsible for a static quality that pervades his works when compared to the more spontaneous Schimmel. His output was small—only a few dozen pieces—and he did his best work as a young man, while still under Schimmel's influence. After years of trying to work unsuccessful farms, Mountz's mental health deteriorated, and he died in the same almshouse as his mentor.

The Peaceable Kingdom of the Serene Leopard. Edward Hicks (1770–1849).
Oil on canvas. 26″ x 29½″. 1846. Bucks County, Pa. Private collection.
Photograph courtesy of the Museum of American Folk Art

In this late *Peaceable Kingdom,* Hicks crowds his canvas with animals and
figures that are arranged symbolically rather than realistically. The wolf,
usually placed in a corner in most of his paintings, is now in the center of
the canvas. The lion cub might have been based on a popular engraving,
published in 1825, of a pair of rare cubs that were bred from a tiger and
a lion.

Noah's Ark
Edward Hicks (1770–1849)
Oil on canvas
26″ x 30″
1848
Bucks County, Pa.
Courtesy of the Philadelphia
Museum of Art

In *Noah's Ark* Hicks painted
animals that hadn't appeared
in his various *Peaceable
Kingdom*s. The lion at the
painting's center is a
self-portrait of Hicks.

EDWARD HICKS (1770–1849)

In addition to its rich legacy of decorative arts and sculptural traditions, Pennsylvania also can claim its Quaker native son Edward Hicks as the most admired folk painter in America. Famous for his many versions of *The Peaceable Kingdom,* Hicks reworked a basic theme of love and religious unity, as expressed in the Vision of Isaiah, using animals as actors in a high drama. Experts estimate that Hicks might have painted as many as one hundred versions, with over sixty pictures finished between 1820 and 1849.[35] Divided into three periods by many historians, Hicks's *Peaceable Kingdom*s show a progression of styles based on artistic growth and emotional expression. By 1830 Hicks introduced many more animals into his canvases, making them larger than the pictured child. Working from illustrated Bibles, paintings, and various engravings, he was probably influenced by such works as M. Anderson's *A General History of Quadrupeds* and Peter Parley's *Tales of Animals.*

Hicks's animals, however, are more than mere copies from prints, as their expressive faces are taut with anxiety or relaxed and serene. The lion and the leopard, often thought to be self-portraits of Hicks, gaze intently with expressions that change over the years. Whether sullen, fierce, or tranquil, they never fail to capture the viewer's attention. Hicks painted the lion in a variety of stances, always placing him in a prominent position. In posing his lions, Hicks probably was influenced by heraldic lions he had seen and by illustrations of lions in various Bibles as well as in paintings and prints. He must have seen a signboard featuring a standing lion advertising the Red Lion Inn of Bucks County. Undoubtedly mirroring the moods of Hicks himself, the lion in various pictures expresses ferocity, sadness, and finally a calm acceptance. Hicks saw the lion as a symbol of the struggle between good and evil. However, it is said that he "loved the spotted leopard best, and often put him spread out on the foreground like a magnificent rug."[36]

Hicks painted his kingdoms against a personal background of emotional turmoil. As a young man he joined the Society of Friends, becoming a minister in 1812. A schism among the Quakers deeply disturbed him and was reflected in his paintings. He considered his *Peaceable Kingdom*s to be "sermons in paint," naively hoping their messages would somehow unite the Quakers.

The artist's precarious financial condition added to his melancholy. A sign painter by trade, he would decorate anything from clock dials to sleds and dog carts in efforts to earn a living. Unlike many craftsmen who had their farms to sustain them, Hicks led a hand-to-mouth existence. His first *Peaceable Kingdom* sold to a neighbor for $25. Its source was a drawing by Richard Westall that appeared as an engraving in English and American Bibles.

During the 1840s, toward the end of his life, Hicks found peace within himself. His animals seem more tranquil, often set in dreamlike, romantic landscapes, suggesting that Hicks at long last had achieved a measure of personal serenity.

"Peaceable Kingdom"
Dr. William Hallowell
Ink on paper
15¾" x 19¾"
c. 1865
New York State
Courtesy of the New York
State Historical Association,
Cooperstown

William Hallowell, a country dentist and a Quaker like Edward Hicks, may have been influenced by the many versions of Hicks's *Peaceable Kingdom,* painted years before Hallowell's drawing.

Snake Quilt
Anonymous
Pieced cottons
76″ x 72″
Late 19th century
North Carolina
Courtesy of Tony and
Marie Shank
Photograph: Ted Whisnant

This heirloom belonged to a black family in the Piedmont area of North Carolina. It is one of the few 19th-century quilts documented as being made by a black woman.

The South

IN THE SOUTH, folk art animals predominate in wood carvings, many made by African slaves and their descendants. Even though most of their work has disappeared, extensive research has established that slaves began creating folk art soon after their arrival in the seventeenth century. Quite naturally their carvings often reflected a heritage of witchcraft, conjuration, and healing. During the 1930s studies by the WPA documented a number of slave artifacts, including a pair of chickens carved in New Orleans (c. 1810–15) by a slave belonging to the pirate Jean Lafitte.[37] It is thought that the important role of the cock in African mythology might have influenced this piece.

Although few such sculptural works of art exist today, a good number of nine-

Root Snake
Anonymous
Painted wood with glass
bead eyes
54″ length
c. 1860
Schohaire County, N.Y.
Collection of
George and Carol Henry
Photograph courtesy of
David A. Schorsch,
New York City

This unknown artist selected
a root for its natural beauty,
then refined it by carving,
sanding, polishing, and
painting. Note the final
touch: glass eyes.

teenth-century walking sticks have been saved. These examples, along with later canes, abound with animals and reptiles found in the lexicon of the African spirit world. Snakes coil around canes offering protection from evil spirits while frogs and lizards create magical spells. Traditional African belief holds that witches living in the form of animals, such as owls and black cats, can wreak havoc upon unfortunate persons.[38] To this day in the deep South there are those who fashion canes that appease the spirits with the appropriate animal symbols. A growing tourist interest beginning in the late nineteenth century added additional incentives for the carving of these canes. Numerous alligator walking sticks from Florida were one response to this demand. However, many walking sticks were also made for the use of family and friends.

As a sad accompaniment to the Civil War, a group of carvings made by soldiers and prisoners-of-war records the anguish of the period. Comprised chiefly of pipe bowls and walking sticks, many contain animal figures. Patriotic symbols such as the eagle predominate, along with serpents and lizards. A few contain hunting scenes with deer, suggesting memories of happier days.

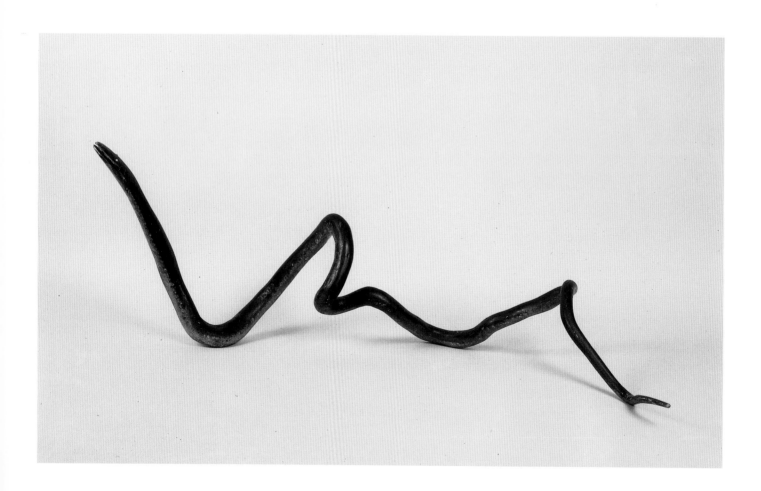

Work Table
Anonymous
Painted poplar
28¾″ x 31½″ x 26½″
Dated 1854
Cherokee County, N.C.
Courtesy of Tony and
Marie Shank
Photograph: Ted Whisnant

Nancy Stalcup, a Cherokee
Indian who originally owned
this table, sold it for $25 in
1896.

Wagon Toolbox
Anonymous
Painted southern pine
28″ x 14″
Early 19th century
Tennessee
Courtesy of
Tony and Marie Shank
Photograph: Ted Whisnant

The Eighteenth and Nineteenth Centuries / 107

Dove Peace Cane. Captain Cleaveland. Whale ivory and baleen.
Cane: 36″ height. Dove: 6″ length. 1865. Massachusetts.
Courtesy of Barbara Johnson, Esq. Photograph: Clem Fiori

Captain Cleaveland began carving this cane during the early
peace talks at the end of the Civil War and finished it as a
celebration of victory.

Animal Cane. Anonymous. Carved and polychromed wood.
35″ height. Dated 1905. Courtesy of Allan Katz

The rhinoceros chases an elephant . . . who chases a bear . . .
who chases a lion . . . who chases a hyena . . . who chases a man
killing a snake. And above them all three men are fighting.

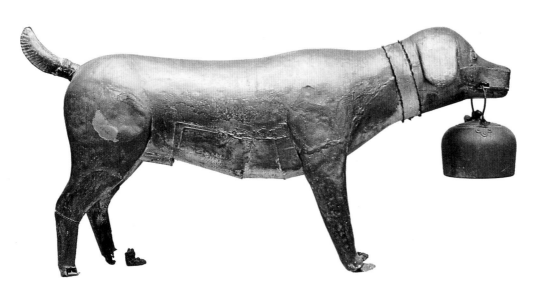

Dogs and Cats

O F A L L the animals depicted by eighteenth- and nineteenth-century folk artists, few were as cherished as America's favorite pets—dogs and cats. Throughout the country painters, sculptors, quilters, rug hookers, whittlers, and metalworkers applied their many talents to portraying canines and felines.

In the colonies dogs held special value because of their hunting abilities. Newspapers of the day advertised dog collars and carried notices of lost dogs. All sorts of periodicals attested to the fidelity and intelligence of dogs. One magazine went so far as to report the comings and goings of its favorite citizen:

> In the ancient and beautiful town of Chatham, N.Y. is a very remarkable dog, whose character and behavior would excite the admiration of all good men. On weekdays, he is a dog with like passions and behavior with other animals, but on Sunday his peculiarities and sectarian prejudices shine out. Unlike the crow, he can count, and knows when Sunday comes.
>
> The family are all Presbyterians, but the dog is a Methodist. On Sunday mornings he attends the family on their way to church, leaves them at the door of the house of the Lord where they attend, and then goes his solitary and unbroken way, till he comes to the Methodist Church. . . . When he reaches the church, he goes upstairs and has a particular place in which he sits . . . and his denominational prejudices are as well known as those of any gentleman in town.[39]

One nineteenth-century gentleman eulogized his dog in the county circuit court of Warrensburg, Missouri: "The most absolutely unselfish friend that man

Girl in Red Dress with Cat and Dog. Ammi Phillips (1788–1865). Oil on canvas. 32″ x 25″. 1834–36. Probably Amenia area, N.Y. Courtesy of the Museum of American Folk Art

The cat may have center stage in this famous painting by Ammi Phillips, but the dog steals the show as he peeks out from behind his young mistress's dress. Similar dogs appear in other portraits of children by Phillips.

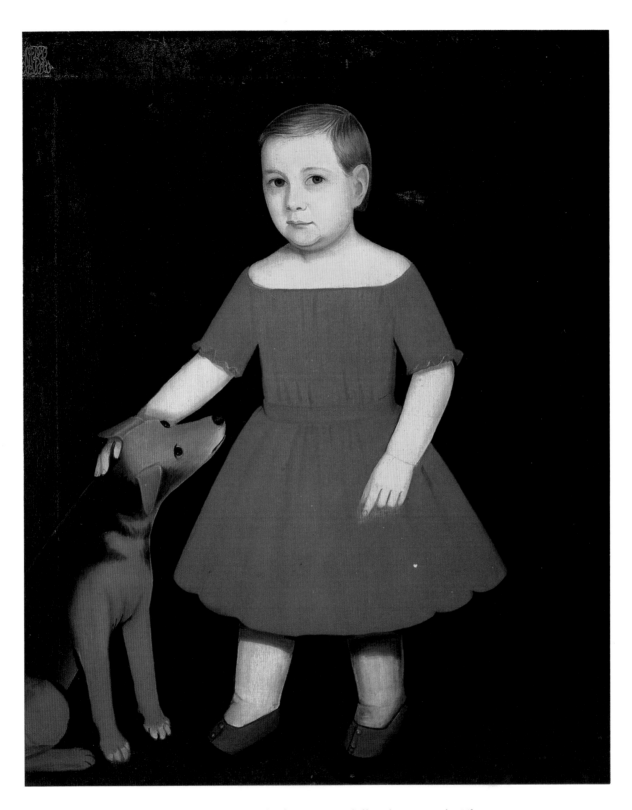

Portrait of Milo Barnum Richardson. Ammi Phillips (1788–1865). Oil on canvas. 33½″ x 27½″. c. 1852. Connecticut. Courtesy of Christie's, New York City

The dog in this portrait is the largest in all of Ammi Phillips's paintings.

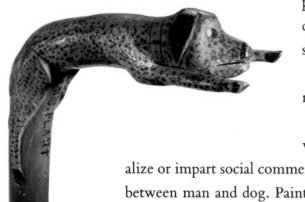

Dog Cane for "Mrs. Plant"
Anonymous
Painted wood
43″ height
19th century
Berry, Vt.
Courtesy of Brian Windsor,
Staten Island, N.Y.
Photograph:
Edward Shoffstall

can have in this selfish world, the one that never proves ungrateful or treacherous, is his dog. A man's dog stands by him in prosperity and in poverty, and in sickness."

Small wonder that dogs are the most depicted animals in the annals of American folk art.

Dogs seem to have especially appealed to the whittler, whose carvings made little attempt to moralize or impart social commentary. They were largely monuments to the affection between man and dog. Paintings of dogs, however, often had dual roles. When included in portraits of children, dogs or cats could distract from an unschooled artist's awkwardness, while adding a sweetness to the picture. They also were part of the "sacred Romantic triad of family, home, and pets . . . fulfilling the nineteenth century's sense of the moral and didactic responsibility of art. . . ."[40] As symbols of the home, cats are often shown sleeping or eating in front of the hearth. Cats were allowed into the home before dogs were granted the privilege. Until the beginning of the twentieth century most dogs were relegated to the yard, except for a few pampered breeds. Gradually over the years the close but changing relationship between Americans and their dogs and cats was revealed by the types of paintings and sculpture that folk artists created. By the twentieth century dogs as hunters and cats as mousers were outnumbered by more domestic scenes.

In many folk paintings cats convey an air of mystery. They are often pictured hiding, and when depicted in a frontal pose, their luminous eyes unremittingly stare at the viewer. In portraits of children many more girls than boys are shown holding cats, just as boys are more frequently shown with dogs and toy horses. Especially appealing are paintings portraying kittens and puppies: kittens frolicking with a ball of yarn or lapping up a bowl of milk, and a female dog nursing her puppies.

ABOVE:
"Trip" Owned by
Robert Newsome
Anonymous
Reverse painting on glass
21½" x 39"
Probably 1890–1900
Saxonville, Mass.
Courtesy of
Samuel Pennington

A rare tinsel painting of a
prized pet. Note on Trip's
collar the touch of gold
leaf and Trip's address,
"R. Newsome, No. 126
Saxonville," in script.

RIGHT:
Seated Dog Sculpture
Anonymous
Painted wood
Dimensions unavailable
Possibly 18th century
Courtesy of Mr. and Mrs.
Kenneth Hammitt
Photograph: Ray Scoury

A primitive, atavistic sculpture. This expression is
sometimes seen in early
American pottery.

Dog Painting
Henry Putney
Watercolor
5¾″ x 7″
19th century
Courtesy of Mr. and Mrs.
Kenneth Hammitt
Photograph: Ray Scoury

Two Whippets
Anonymous
Watercolor and calligraphy
15¾″ x 13″
Courtesy of Mr. and Mrs.
Kenneth Hammitt
Photograph: Ray Scoury

Calligraphy and watercolor
painting were taught at the
finest 19th-century female
academies. This painting
might have been executed by
a young woman eager to
display both skills.

The Pointer
S. A. Payton
Oil on canvas
12″ x 20½″
1819
Courtesy of Lillian and
Jerry Grossman

Painting of Child with Dog
William Matthew Prior
(1806–1873)
Oil on canvas
27″ x 27″
1845
Marblehead, Mass.
Courtesy of the Artvest
Collection

It is believed that a ship
captain commissioned
William Matthew Prior
to paint his daughter and
her pet dog. Note the harbor
through the window.

Portrait of Tom
Ella Wood
Oil on canvas
18½" x 15"
c. 1865
Guilford, N.H.
Collection of Robert Wagner
Photograph courtesy of
David A. Schorsch,
New York City

Cat Needlework Picture
Anonymous
Woolen threads sewn on
punched paper
14″ x 12¼″
c. 1880
New England
Courtesy of Kathy Schoemer,
North Salem, N.Y.
Photograph: Mike Levins

A Victorian craft, punched-
paper needlework might be
called the forerunner of
paint-by-number kits.

Cat Pincushion
Anonymous
Wool, cotton, and silk ribbon
6″ x 7″
c. 1880–90
Lancaster, Pa.
Courtesy of Richard and
Betty Ann Rasso,
East Chatham, N.Y.

In Pennsylvania, decorated
pincushions often hung from
shelves of corner and Dutch
cupboards or were placed in
china cabinets.

Theorem. Anonymous. Paint on velvet. 21¾″ x 26″. 19th century. Courtesy of Judy and John Angelo

Except for still lifes with parrots, theorems (a school-girl art) rarely contain animals. Yet the cat here with its fluffy tail is a prominent part of an otherwise traditional scene.

THE TWENTIETH CENTURY

T HE WORK of many early folk artists remains anonymous, but twentieth-century art is enriched by the documentation of artists' lives. As a result of mass communication, few contemporary artists remain unknown. In fact, almost all twentieth-century folk art can be identified as to artist and place. When anecdotal material is accessible, it reveals *why* and *how* people painted, sculpted, and carved the many animals found in contemporary American folk art.

The variety of twentieth-century folk animals manifests a tremendous energy, reflecting lives completely preoccupied with art, although the makers themselves often had no formal training. A compulsive need for self-expression, sometimes the result of inner visions and dreams, brought out creative activity. In talking about E. A. McKillop, a North Carolina artist who in 1926 began carving animals after receiving a gift of three or four black walnut trees in exchange for cutting them down, his daughter Lelia noted:

> It was just in him, it was just in him. He didn't take any schooling; he didn't take any training. And he never done any carving until he just got that wood. And he just went to work on it, and he just turned out all these things. It was just in him—just talented. That's all you can say.[1]

Many relatives of twentieth-century folk artists have been hard pressed to explain their kin's talent. And the artists themselves sometimes don't offer much additional information. When McKillop was asked by admirers of his menagerie, "Well, how do you get this all in your mind?" he'd say, "Well, you just eat a big mess of fatback and go to bed and go to sleep and dream how to do it."[2]

The Getaway
Horace Pippin (1888–1946)
Oil on canvas
24″ x 35½″
1939
West Chester, Pa.
Courtesy of the Janet Fleisher
Gallery, Philadelphia

Painted on the eve of World
War II.

Prancing Horses
Lawrence Lebduska
(1894–1966)
Oil on canvas
21″ x 25″
1937
Baltimore, Md.
Courtesy of the Museum of
American Folk Art

Lebduska has often been
compared to the Fauvists in
France. Here, as in most
of his paintings, his horses
prance and frolic in an
idyllic landscape.

Cat Quilt. Anonymous. Cotton, feed sacks, and muslin. 82½″ x 66½″.
1930–40. Kentucky. Courtesy of the Museum of American Folk Art, Gift
of Laura Fisher. Photograph: Schecter Lee

Three Turkeys
Anonymous
Iron and brass
6¼″ x 5″ each
1910
Massachusetts
Courtesy of
Barbara Johnson, Esq.
Photograph: Clem Fiori

Target Birds
Anonymous
Painted iron
13½″ x 12¼″
1920s
New York
Courtesy of
Barbara Johnson, Esq.
Photograph: Clem Fiori

Cow-Head Folk Sculpture
Anonymous
Painted metal and wood
14″ height
Early 20th century
Mississippi
Courtesy of Aarne Anton,
New York City

Originally this cow mask
hung on a barn in rural
Mississippi. It was made by
an unknown black artist.

Pink Bear Hooked Rug
Anonymous
Wool and cotton on burlap
23″ x 33″
1910
Illinois
Courtesy of
Barbara Johnson, Esq.
Photograph: Clem Fiori

The use of cotton yarns
occurred only in the 20th
century.

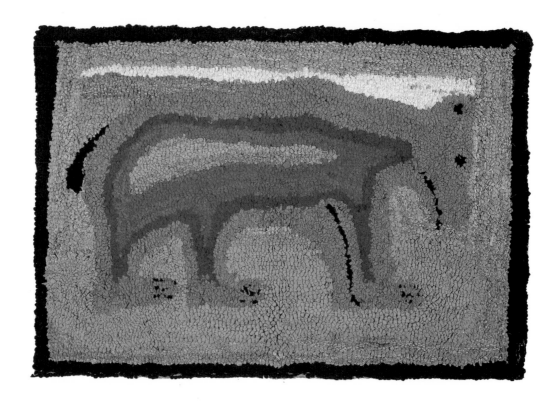

"Pick of the Litter"
Hooked Rug
Anonymous
Wool on burlap
38½″ x 21″
1950s
Courtesy of
Barbara Johnson, Esq.
Photograph: Clem Fiori

Note that the mother pig
dominates and is outlined in
black, while the piglets are
not as well defined.

Bluebird Hooked Rug
Anonymous
Wool on burlap
40″ x 32″
1930s
Ohio
Courtesy of
Barbara Johnson, Esq.
Photograph: Clem Fiori

"Cleopatra" Hooked Rug
Anonymous
Wool and rayon on burlap
44½″ x 33″
1930
Connecticut
Courtesy of
Barbara Johnson, Esq.
Photograph: Clem Fiori

Barbara Johnson named this
rug "Cleopatra" because of
the animal's wonderful mane.

Silver Bird
Anonymous
Carved wood painted silver
9″ x 12½″
c. 1930s
Courtesy of Aarne Anton,
New York City

Clearly, the design of this
bird was influenced by the
Art Deco movement. Note
the sleekness often found in
sculpture of that period.

Ornamental Water Handle
Anonymous
Cast in bronze
7″ x 7″
c. 1930
Eastern United States
Courtesy of Aarne Anton,
New York City

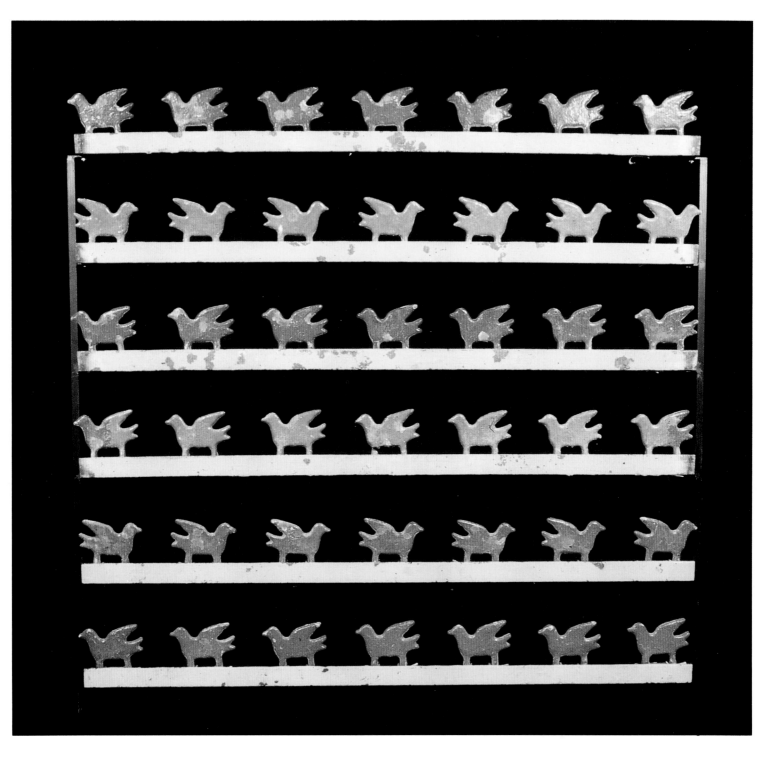

Birds Shooting Gallery. Anonymous. Painted metal. 42″ x 44″. 1930s.
New York State. Courtesy of Aarne Anton, New York City

Sheep Sculpture
Stephen Huneck (b. 1948)
Bronze
2′ x 3′ x 6″
1988
Johnsbury, Vt.
Courtesy of Stephen Huneck

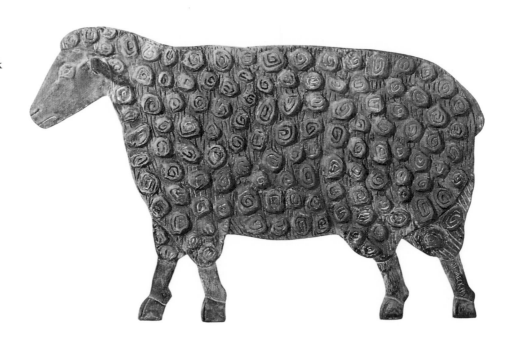

Lion Painting
Joseph Gatto (1893–1965)
Oil on board
48″ x 36″
1940s
New York City
Courtesy of the
Epstein-Powell Gallery,
New York City

Joseph Gatto lived in New York City, making a living doing odd jobs. His jungle scenes have been compared to those of the French primitive Henri Rousseau. Less idealized than Rousseau's paintings, Gatto's work displays an intensity and an emotional power. When told of the comparison Gatto responded, "I went to look at that Rousseau they're talking about. The guy's been stealing my stuff for years."

King Tut Challace. Rev. Benjamin F. Perkins. Paint on canvas. 34½″ x 22½″.
1988. Fayette County, Ala. Courtesy of the Tartt Gallery, Washington, D.C.

Perkins, a retired Marine and a fundamentalist minister, began to paint in
1977, "to keep from sitting down and doing nothing." His artistic efforts
are divided between painting gourds that he grows on his land in Alabama
and painting colorful canvases filled with rich geometric patterns.

Afro-American Mule Quilt. Betty Rogers. Cotton. 72½″ x 70″. 1988.
Alabama. Courtesy of the Robert Cargo Folk Art Gallery, Tuscaloosa, Ala.

The embroidered eyes resemble field daisies.

Noah's Ark Quilt. Yvonne Wells. Quilted cotton. 74″ x 77″. 1988.
Tuscaloosa, Ala. Courtesy of the Robert Cargo Folk Art Gallery,
Tuscaloosa, Ala.

This colorful piece with its interesting asymmetrical composition is typical
of many Afro-American quilts.

Horse Windmill Weight
Dempster Mill
Manufacturing Co.
Painted cast iron
18½″ x 18″
Early 20th century
Beatrice, Nebr.
Courtesy of Sidney Gecker,
New York City

By the 1880s almost every
self-respecting farm or ranch
employed a windmill, each
boasting a functional yet
decorative windmill weight.
Horses were among the most
popular forms, with some
weights resembling
weathervanes.

"Two Arabian Horses"
William Dawson (b. 1901)
Paint on masonite
12¾″ x 19″
1982
Chicago, Ill.
Private collection
Photograph courtesy of the
Phylis Kind Galleries,
Chicago and New York City

William Dawson began
painting and sculpting when
he retired in the mid-1960s.
His work is about his
childhood on an Alabama
farm.

Rabbit Lap Robe. Labeled "Chase". Wool. 4′ x 5′. c. 1900. Cullman, Ala.
Courtesy of the Robert Cargo Folk Art Gallery, Tuscaloosa, Ala.

Outsider Art

SOME OF the most striking work featuring animals has been created by artists working outside the mainstream of the art world. Appropriately known as "Outsiders" or "Isolates," these men and women exhibit a tenacity and independence that is reflected in their unique animal forms. Many of these artists hold an animistic view of the universe, seeing animals or parts of animals in inanimate objects. Artists choose what superficially appears to be a random selection of wood, metal, or wire, visualizing the shape of the animal before they begin to assemble, paint, or sculpt. Until recently outsider art was usually ignored by the art world. Today, however, galleries, museums, and art enthusiasts eagerly seek out new artists and material from this group. Although outsider artists can be found in both rural and urban areas, many artists focusing on animals are Afro-Americans working in the deep South. Their sculptures and paintings deliberately or unconsciously reflect their visual ties to an Afro-American heritage rich in animal lore. Monkeys, rep-

OPPOSITE PAGE: Giraffe.
Gregorio Marzan (b. 1906).
Mixed media. 24″ x 39″.
c. 1978. New York City.
Courtesy of El Museo del Barrio.
Photograph: Dawoud Bey

Originally from Puerto Rico,
Marzan moved in 1937 to
New York City, where he
worked at various factories
making toys and dolls until
his retirement in 1971.
Experimenting with small
sculptures of birds and houses
in the late 1970s, Marzan
developed a unique style and
created a virtual menagerie of
fanciful creatures.

tiles, birds, and fish are rooted in tales of witchcraft and conjuration, still told in some southern rural communities. The power of such folklore is intensified by the cultural and economic isolation experienced in the South, resulting in a body of animal sculpture characterized by the visions of fevered imaginations.

Vulture Painting
William Dawson (b. 1901)
Oil on cardboard
11″ x 15″
1983
Chicago, Ill.
Courtesy of the
Epstein-Powell Gallery,
New York City
Photograph: D. James Dee

Dawson is one of the few 20th-century folk artists to work in both painting and sculpture.

Horse and Jockey
Justin McCarthy (1891–1977)
Oil on board
16″ x 23¾″
c. 1960
Weatherly, Pa.
Courtesy of the Museum of American Folk Art

Justin McCarthy began to paint as a young man while in a mental institution. This picture exhibits many aspects of his later work, including an intense palette, jagged lines, and bigger-than-life compositions.

Two Roosters. Emma Lee Moss (b. 1916). Acrylic on board. 18″ x 24″. 1984.
Dallas, Tex. Courtesy of the Epstein-Powell Gallery, New York City.
Photograph: D. James Dee

Emma Lee Moss has painted in different mediums on many surfaces,
including window shades and shoe boxes (for Neiman-Marcus specifically).
"All I want to do is paint a picture I like . . ."

Snake Collage
Simon Sparrow (b. 1925)
Paint, beads, and glitter
17½″ x 21½″
1980s
Madison, Wis.
Courtesy of Bert Hemphill
Photograph:
Edward Shofstall

Simon Sparrow, a West
African brought to North
Carolina at age two, has
always been influenced by
African spiritualism. It is
believed the heavy beading
and glittering surfaces of his
collages are tied to early black
funeral customs.

"Red Dog"
Clyde Jones (b. 1938)
Painted wood
19″ x 28″
1986
North Carolina
Courtesy of the MIA Gallery,
Seattle, Wash.

Clyde Jones has created
several hundred animals
using suggestive root
fragments, gourds, found
objects, and brilliant paints,
many of which he keeps in
his ever-expanding yard.

Saw Owl Sculpture
Norman Scott "Butch"
Quinn
Mixed media on hand saw
26″ x 7″
1988
Pennsylvania
Courtesy of the Tartt Gallery,
Washington, D.C.

Butch Quinn revels in
transforming ordinary
household objects into
conveyors of his personal
dreams and feelings.

"White Mane Lion"
William Hawkins (b. 1895)
Enamel on paper
35″ x 38″
1980s
Columbus, Ohio
Courtesy of the Janet Fleisher
Gallery, Philadelphia

Black Bull
William Hawkins (b. 1895)
Enamel on masonite
48″ square
c. 1984
Columbus, Ohio
Courtesy of the Janet Fleisher
Gallery, Philadelphia

This anthropomorphic bull is
typical of Hawkins's many
animal paintings.

"Elephants". William Hawkins (b. 1895). Enamel on board. 47″ x 38″. 20th century. Columbus, Ohio. Private collection. Photograph courtesy of the Janet Fleisher Gallery, Philadelphia

William Hawkins's animals are large, colorful creatures. Hawkins, favoring primary colors, paints in large brushstrokes, intent on capturing the essence of the animal.

Raccoon Cane. Sam Martin (b. 1926). Baywood and red cedar. 41″ length. 1987. Shelby County, Ala. Courtesy of the Robert Cargo Folk Art Gallery, Tuscaloosa, Ala.

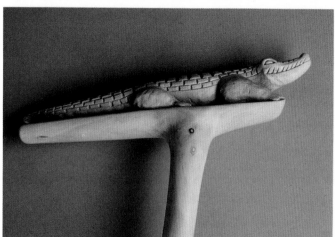

Alligator Cane. Sam Martin (b. 1926). Sourwood. 39½″ length. 1986. Shelby County, Ala. Courtesy of the Robert Cargo Folk Art Gallery, Tuscaloosa, Ala.

Martin came from a family of carvers. His grandfather taught his father, who in turn passed on his skills to his son. Martin's finely carved alligator is polished to a patina of ivory.

Cougar Cane. Sam Martin (b. 1926). Carved sourwood. 39½″ length. 1986. Shelby County, Ala. Courtesy of the Robert Cargo Folk Art Gallery, Tuscaloosa, Ala.

Sam Martin makes small animals, canes, and whimseys. Here he used only a pocketknife to carve the cat from one piece of wood. He sanded it to a smooth finish, and applied a coat of paste wax to give the cane an appearance of antique ivory.

"Janet Munro on Zebra"
Justin McCarthy (1891–1977)
India ink on paper
22″ x 28″
1961
Weatherly, Pa.
Courtesy of the Cavin-Morris
Slide Archives

Throughout most of his
forty-year career, Justin
McCarthy was unappreciated;
his work wasn't acknowl-
edged until 1960.

Zebra Painting
Justin McCarthy (1891–1977)
Oil on board
18″ x 11″
c. 1960
Weatherly, Pa.
Courtesy of the
Epstein-Powell Gallery,
New York City
Photograph: D. James Dee

The soft, expressive strokes of
Justin McCarthy impart a
gentleness to his portrait of a
young zebra. Typical of most
McCarthy animal paintings,
the zebra dominates the
visual field.

"The only Real Life I know
is God in my soul through
Jesus"
Rev. Howard Finster (b. 1916)
Enamel on wood
Approximately 21″ x 25″
1988
Pennville, Ga.
Courtesy of the
Phylis Kind Galleries,
Chicago and New York City

"The Great American Cheata"
Rev. Howard Finster (b. 1916)
Enamel on wood
13″ x 17¼″
1986
Pennville, Ga.
Private collection
Photograph courtesy of the
Phylis Kind Galleries,
Chicago and New York City

Finster's work has been
characterized as "sermons in
paint," which accurately
reflects the driving force
behind them.

Elephant Sculpture
Ralph Griffin (b. 1925)
Painted tree stump
10″ x 6″ x 5″
1988
North-central Georgia
Courtesy of the Tartt Gallery,
Washington, D.C.

Ralph Griffin uses a simple
tree stump: he finds in it,
and then refines, the
quintessential animal, which
he paints.

"Leopard on Green"
Charles Kinney (b. 1906)
Tempera on paper
22″ x 28″
1986
Vanceburg, Ky.
Courtesy of the MIA Gallery,
Seattle, Wash.

Charles Kinney and his
brother, Noah, are said to be
"keepers of old time ways
and lore." "Haints, tokens,
and knocking spirits" were
very real to Charles as a child,
and he frequently depicts
old-time spooky tales and
animals.

Baboon Sculpture
Elijah Pierce (b. 1892)
Enamel and glitter on wood
7½″ x 8″
1980
Columbus, Ohio
Courtesy of the Gasperi Folk
Art Gallery, New Orleans
Photograph: Gerald Murrell

Elijah Pierce often imbues an
individual animal with the
characteristics of other
species. Here, the baboon
displays markedly bovine
features.

Elephant Sculpture
William Dawson (b. 1901)
Polychromed wood
11″ x 7¼″ x 2″
1986
Chicago, Ill.
Private collection
Photograph courtesy of the
Phylis Kind Galleries,
Chicago and New York City

Snake Sculpture
Michael Finster
Painted and carved wood
11½″ x 12″ x 6″
1987
Pennville, Ga.
Courtesy of the Tartt Gallery,
Washington, D.C.

Fish Swimming with Snakes
Thorton Dial (b. 1928)
Painted metal
11″ x 28″
1988
Sumter County, Ala.
Courtesy of the Tartt Gallery,
Washington, D.C.

Thorton Dial and several of
his sons and nephews work
with scrap cast iron, car-body
repair material, and other
found objects. Seeing his
work at the High Museum
(in Atlanta) in their
exhibition *Outside the
Mainstream: Folk Art in Our
Time* in 1988, Dial put his
hand over his heart and said,
"When I saw my work
displayed, I was overcome."

Pig Painting
Bill Traylor (1854–1947)
Showcard color on cardboard
10″ x 14½″
c. 1940
Montgomery, Ala.
Courtesy of the Luise Ross
Gallery, New York City

Cat Painting
Bill Traylor (1854–1947)
Gouache on cardboard
7″ x 13″
1939–41
Montgomery, Ala.
Courtesy of the Cavin-Morris
Slide Archives

Bull Painting
Bill Traylor (1854–1947)
Showcard color on cardboard
11″ x 15″
c. 1940
Montgomery, Ala.
Private collection
Photograph courtesy of the
Luise Ross Gallery,
New York City

The splitting of animals into
two distinct areas of color
appears frequently in Plains
Indian hide and ledger
paintings. It is certain that
Traylor knew nothing of
their work.

BILL TRAYLOR (1854–1947)

Bill Traylor, an ex-slave, is seen as a bridge between African ritual images and modern art. His animals are boldly defined, filled with areas of pure color. The rules of perspective did not interest Traylor. His animals often appear to tower over the human figures walking or tending them. Traylor never revealed his reasons for his preoccupation with animals, just as he didn't explain much about his art. When working he held his pencil in one hand and a small stick in the other hand, which he used for measuring.

Devotees of Traylor have surmised that his life among farm animals affected his choice of subject, just as his Afro-American heritage subconsciously influenced his style. Many people see a link between Traylor's work and African ritual figures. Robert Cargo, a folk art historian and dealer, believes there is a connection between the use of suspended figures in Traylor's pictures and those found in two biblical, appliqué quilts by Harriet Powers, an ex-slave working in Athens, Georgia, in the late nineteenth century. Similar arrangements of figures appear in traditional African appliqué fabrics. Many of Traylor's drawings portray animals of totemic significance to Africans: chickens, lions, large felines, and bulls.[3] His animals also have been compared to ancient creatures painted on prehistoric cave walls as well as to animals depicted in ancient Egyptian art.

Paradoxes are partly responsible for the fascination with the purple pig, the fero-

Rabbit Painting
Bill Traylor (1854–1947)
Tempera and graphite on
cardboard
7½″ x 10″
c. 1939
Montgomery, Ala.
Private collection
Photograph courtesy of the
Cavin-Morris Gallery

cious dog, and the balking mule of Bill Traylor. One is never certain what these animals represent—they puzzle us while delighting us at the same time. In one sense they are straightforward, painted in pure primary colors (Traylor never mixed his paints), but in another sense they are mysterious, painted in uneven strokes and drawn with sharp jagged lines.

Traylor's period of productivity was short (he did not start drawing until he was eighty-five), but, working at a feverish pitch, he created between one and two thousand images before entering a nursing home in Montgomery, Alabama, shortly before his death in 1947 at the age of ninety-three.

Goat
Bill Traylor (1854–1947)
Poster paint on cardboard
7¾″ x 8¾″
c. 1940
Montgomery, Ala.
Courtesy of the
Luise Ross Gallery,
New York City

MOSE TOLLIVER (b. 1919)

Like Bill Traylor, Mose Tolliver is a southern, Afro-American painter known for his many animal paintings. Also like Traylor, Tolliver did not begin to paint until late in life. After his foot was crushed in an accident, Tolliver started experimenting with painting in the 1970s. He painted what interested him, mostly animals, people, and landscapes, often repeating a subject over and over again. However, many of Tolliver's fans feel that his genius lies in his ability to invent new forms within the framework of the same image. While Tolliver has painted literally thousands of what is known as the "Tolliver Bird," no two are exactly alike. Rather, they are endless variations on a theme. Robert Cargo, who has sold many Tolliver paintings, notes: "The colors will change, the bird here will be surrounded by strange spots of color like so many falling flakes of brightly colored snow, here pecking at an exotic flower, or else perched on the branch of some strange tree, again with a clutch of vividly colored eggs, or else with a chick or two, or shown under a strange tree, both the tree and bird in bizarrely marbleized colors, or ready to attack a piece of real bone that has been attached to the board as in a collage."[4]

A few of Tolliver's animals were inspired by illustrations in children's books; others were his own inventions. The fact that he gave some of his animal paintings names such as "Quail Fish" and "Frog Birds" suggests a desire to combine aspects of various species in one image. Bill Traylor also combined two animals in a painting. Although Tolliver did not know Traylor's work firsthand, he does own a well-thumbed copy of *Black Folk Art in America, 1930–1980,* in which Traylor's work is represented.[5]

Tolliver's paintings are easy to recognize—he employs a stylized approach with distinctive painted borders around his pictures. Using ordinary house paint bought by the gallon, he will work on anything available, be it cardboard, plywood, gourds, sections of tree trunks, or even the back of an upholstered chair. By mixing paint directly on the painting itself, Tolliver achieves the desired shades and nuances, creating a harmonious palette that enhances a feeling of fantasy. His animals fill the space of whatever medium he chooses, appearing larger than life even though his paintings are small. Due to his reliance on crutches, Tolliver can only paint while seated. The size of a painting is determined by what he can hold on his lap as he sits on the edge of his bed, turning the painting as it progresses—now top up, now top down, sideways—because he always pulls the brush toward his body.

Tolliver's animals are often thought of as possessing dreamlike qualities, especially his pastel fantasies. His more realistic depictions in bright colors exude energy and appear to be a celebration of life.

Snake and Turtle Painting
Mose Tolliver (b. 1919)
Paint on wood
27″ x 18″
1986
Montgomery, Ala.
Courtesy of the MIA Gallery,
Seattle, Wash.

Owl Painting
Mose Tolliver (b. 1919)
Paint on wood
24″ x 24″
1988
Montgomery, Ala.
Courtesy of the Tartt Gallery,
Washington, D.C.

Tolliver painted a frame
around his painting; it saved
money and reflects his make-
do philosophy.

Bird Painting
Mose Tolliver (b. 1919)
House paint on board
17½″ x 18½″
1987
Montgomery, Ala.
Courtesy of the Robert Cargo
Folk Art Gallery,
Tuscaloosa, Ala.

It is said that Mose Tolliver
studied only a couple of birds
before he began to paint
them. Tolliver drew simple
shapes that defied laws of
proportion. His birds became,
as he said, "like no birds that
ever drew breath."

Rooster Painting. Jimmie Lee Sudduth (b. 1910). House paint on board.
18″ x 18″. 1986. Fayette County, Ala. Courtesy of the Epstein-Powell
Gallery, New York City. Photograph: D. James Dee

Sudduth has begun to omit dirt from his paint mixture, but he still continues
to use earthy colors with texture.

Fighting Horses
Jimmie Lee Sudduth (b. 1910)
Oil and dirt on board
18″ x 24″
1986
Fayette County, Ala.
Courtesy of the
Epstein-Powell Gallery,
New York City
Photograph: D. James Dee

JIMMIE LEE SUDDUTH (b. 1910)

Jimmie Lee Sudduth, an Afro-American artist, born and still living in the New Canaan community of Fayette County, Alabama, has been painting animals for as long as he can remember. Sudduth has created a veritable animal kingdom with his representations of snakes, turtles, and alligators; rabbits, deer, quail, wild turkeys, and squirrels; ducks, geese, chickens, and eagles. While he has painted many dogs, he has rarely portrayed cats. His interest in dogs probably stems from the several who seem always to hang around his yard. His own, a long-haired white dog, Toto (named for Toto in *The Wizard of Oz*), has served as a model for many of his dog paintings. His few fish are particularly fine, as are his horses, cows, and dinosaurs. In the insect world he has chosen to paint a spider and a dragonfly, which he calls in typical Alabama fashion a "snakedoctor."[6]

Sudduth is known as "the dirt painter" because of his use of various kinds of dirt from around his house to create shade and color differentiation in his paintings. Dirt is mixed with water; in earlier years it was mixed with sugar. Persuaded to omit sugar because of the preservation problems, Sudduth now just blends natural dyes such as turnip greens with dirt or sometimes submits to the luxury of house paint.

Sudduth's animals are dignified, never cute. They are painted with broad, determined strokes that manifest a raw power. Like Tolliver's subjects, many of Sudduth's animals appear to be larger than life, painted in bright colors. Now acclaimed as one of Alabama's most popular folk artists, Sudduth relishes his new role. "This is something new," Jimmie Lee himself expresses it. "This is somethin' the art people ain't got—in the whole world."[7]

Eagle Painting
Jimmie Lee Sudduth (b. 1910)
House paint and dirt
on board
23½″ x 32″
1986
Fayette County, Ala.
Courtesy of the Robert Cargo
Folk Art Gallery,
Tuscaloosa, Ala.

"Every time I see dirt,"
Jimmie Lee Sudduth has said,
"my mouth waters and I say,
'I need to get some of that.'"

Camel with Rattlesnake
Painting
Jimmie Lee Sudduth (b. 1910)
Paint mixed with dirt
on board
22″ x 23″
1985
Fayette County, Ala.
Courtesy of the Robert Cargo
Folk Art Gallery,
Tuscaloosa, Ala.

"Lion with the Broken Tail"
Nellie Mae Rowe
(1900–1982)
Collage, crayon, and felt-tip
pen on paper
18″ x 24″
1981
Vinings, Ga.
Courtesy of Judith Alexander,
Atlanta

Nellie Mae Rowe didn't feel
the need to sign her name on
the bottom right of her
canvases and here chose a
prominent spot for her
signature and date.

NELLIE MAE ROWE (1900–1982)

Growing up on a farm in Fayette County, Georgia, one of ten children, Nellie Mae Rowe sandwiched making art in between picking cotton and other chores. She drew on scraps of paper, knotted laundry into dolls, and shaped bread dough into figures. Her artistic efforts reappeared after the death of her second husband in 1948 and her retirement from work. Not only did she produce scores of drawings but she also created an "environment" in her yard, hanging dolls, stuffed animals, and found objects on the trees and bushes. She even started making small animal sculptures out of chewed gum. Twice married but childless, Rowe might have been trying to stave off loneliness as she surrounded herself with memories of her childhood. She noted: "When I was a child, I always liked to get a pencil and paper, get down on the floor and draw. It didn't amount to nothing then, but in the long run it did. . . . Now I got to get back to my childhood, what you call playing in a playhouse."[8]

Today Nellie Mae Rowe is known for her Chagall-like paintings of floating mules, bright blue dogs, polka-dotted elephants, butterflies, and myriad birds. A visionary artist, she credited her creative energy to God's plan. Lying awake at night, a shape or object would appear that she later transformed into one of her "fantasies." Working with crayons, colored pencils, felt-tip pens, as well as common pencils and pens, Rowe drew with a strong sense of color and a spirited imagination. Spontaneity formed the core of her art—she was proud that when she took pencil to paper, she often didn't know where it was going to lead her. More often than not animals appear in her drawings, but she never explained her particular fascination with them. When asked what a fish in a picture meant, Rowe replied, "What it is!"

"Red Bird"
Nellie Mae Rowe
(1900–1982)
Gouache and pencil on paper
18″ x 23″
c. 1980
Vinings, Ga.
Collection of Chase
Manhattan Bank
Photograph courtesy of
Judith Alexander, Atlanta

Nellie Mae Rowe's paintings
have frequently been
compared to works by
Marc Chagall.

"Sky Filght" (Flight)
Nellie Mae Rowe
(1900–1982)
Pencil and crayon on paper
19″ x 24″
c. 1979
Vinings, Ga.
Collection of John and
Elizabeth Spiegel
Photograph courtesy of
Judith Alexander, Atlanta

One of Rowe's richest works.

"Green Pig"
Nellie Mae Rowe
(1900–1982)
Crayon on paper
17¾″ x 13¾″
c. 1979
Vinings, Ga.
Private collection
Photograph courtesy of
Judith Alexander, Atlanta

The Twentieth Century / 161

"Chewing Gum Cat"
Nellie Mae Rowe
(1900–1982)
Chewing gum, paint, plastic
flowers, and beads
5½" x 7¾" x 7½"
Undated
Vinings, Ga.
Courtesy of Judith
Alexander, Atlanta

Nellie Mae Rowe began her
chewing gum sculptures
before she had committed
herself to her art on a full-
time basis. Saving her used
gum (she only chewed
spearmint) in a coffee can,
she would shape it into the
desired animal or figure,
harden it in her refrigerator,
and then paint it.

"Fish on Spools"
Nellie Mae Rowe
(1900–1982)
Acrylic on wood
24" x 8"
1980
Fayette County, Ga.
Collection of the
High Museum
Photograph courtesy of
Judith Alexander, Atlanta

As in many of her pictures,
Nellie Mae Rowe paints her
sculpture with a dense
application of color and
covers it with bright dots.

DAVID BUTLER (b. 1898)

David Butler works in sculpture in Patterson, Louisiana, and is often compared to Mose Tolliver. Like Tolliver, Butler is an Afro-American with deep roots to his past. He, too, did not take up what has become his life's work until after he sustained a physical disability. A religious man, Butler explores universal themes through his animal sculptures. He can be compared to Edward Hicks in that they both intended their art to convey spiritual messages. As Hicks surrounded himself with his *Peaceable Kingdom*s, Butler has literally encircled himself with his sculptures, placing them in his yard "as if to ward off unfriendly spirits."[9]

Butler's animals are cut and folded metal assemblages that are brightened by coats of paint. Rainbow-hued, they delight the eye with an easy charm that belies the artist's carefully thought out aesthetic principles. David Butler claims ideas for sculptures come to him in technicolor dreams. After sketching them on pieces of

Ram Sculpture
David Butler (b. 1898)
Enamel on tin
10″ x 17″
c. 1970
Patterson, La.
Courtesy of the Gasperi Folk Art Gallery, New Orleans
Photograph: Gerald Murrell

tin, he cuts them out using a hammer and meat cleaver. "I see them things at night when I lay down, and I get up and cut them out just like I see it."[10]

In spite of his lack of formal education, Butler exhibits a sophisticated approach to his complicated sculptures. They resemble giant jigsaw pieces that somehow fit together to form a unified vision, a Noah's Ark composed of gaily colored "snipped tin." Recurring dual images suggest a preoccupation with the transformation of figures into mythic beings, so that a ship becomes an ark and a fish becomes a mermaid.[11] Some of Butler's sculptures can be compared to fishing decoys enlivened with bits of tinfoil, mirrors, and other attention-getting found objects. Because there is so much to "see" in a Butler sculpture, a wealth of associations with folk art, past and present, come to mind.

"Fierce Fish" Sculpture
David Butler (b. 1898)
Enamel on tin
9¾″ x 16″
Patterson, La.
Courtesy of the Gasperi Folk
Art Gallery, New Orleans
Photograph: Gerald Murrell

Applying broad areas of color balanced by cutouts, Butler contrasts the large area of the body with the tiny, sharp teeth of his aptly named "Fierce Fish."

"Noah's Ark". David Butler (b. 1898). Enamel paint on sheet metal. 28″ x 29″. 1987. Patterson, La. Courtesy of the Epstein-Powell Gallery, New York City. Photograph: D. James Dee

To create his Noah's Ark, David Butler first traced its outline on weathered tin ("It paints better"), then cut out the shape with a meat cleaver and shears and used house paint to finish the sculpture.

Hen with Chicken
David Butler (b. 1898)
Cut and painted tin
9½″ x 15″
c. 1970s
Patterson, La.
Courtesy of the Robert Cargo
Folk Art Gallery,
Tuscaloosa, Ala.

One of David Butler's most
appealing sculptures. The
theme of a baby within its
mother has interested many
folk artists, who have
frequently depicted animals
or fish inside the stomach of
a whale or other predator.

Camel Sculpture
David Butler (b. 1898)
Enamel on tin
10″ x 14″
c. 1970
Patterson, La.
Courtesy of the Gasperi Folk
Art Gallery, New Orleans
Photograph: Gerald Murrell

WILLIAM EDMONDSON (c. 1870–1951)

William Edmondson of Nashville, Tennessee, was one of the few American folk artists to sculpt in stone and the first Afro-American artist to be honored by a one-man show at the Museum of Modern Art in 1937. Edmondson, the son of slaves, worked first as a laborer and then as a janitor for a hospital in Nashville, until it closed in 1931. He was a devoutly religious man. He heard voices and he saw visions, and he believed these visions directed him to take up stonecutting. He wasn't able to afford the tools of a stonemason, so he used a battered hammer and fashioned a chisel from a flattened spike. He began by carving tombstones for people in his church who liked the memorials he had adorned with doves and sheep. Edmondson probably copied these figures from the many doves and sheep he saw on headstones in the graveyard. The lambs were so popular that Sears, Roebuck carried them in their catalogue for as little as $10.[12] Working in limestone, which was cheap and readily available, he gradually started carving "figures," filling his yard with his "miracles" that included a variety of animals—doves, eagles, cranes, frogs, turtles, horses, bears, lions, rabbits, squirrels, and rams. He also made "critters" and "varmints," animal sculptures whose species eluded identification.

Too modest to proclaim himself an artist, Edmondson hung a simple sign over his workshed reading: "Tombstones for sale/garden ornaments/stone work/Wm. Edmondson."[3] His garden ornaments included bird baths featuring the same doves that he made for tombstone finials. Although Edmondson thought of himself as a tombstone carver, his visions led him to the realm of sculpture.

Like many folk carvers Edmondson could *see* his figures within the untouched stone, after first "seeing them in the sky."[4] He worked close to the surface, carving simplified forms, doing away with texture except for occasionally delineating the fur of an animal. While the medium of limestone dictated an abstract approach, Edmondson appeared to embrace it as the perfect vehicle for his art. In his mind he was relaying God's spiritual messages, re-creating in stone God's will. In his own words: "This here stone and all those out there in the yard come from God. It's the work of Jesus speaking His mind in my mind. I must be one of his disciples. These here is miracles I can do. Can't nobody do these but me. I can't help carving. I just does it. It's like when you're leaving here you're going home. Well, I know I'm going to carve. Jesus has planted the seed of carving in me."[5]

Edmondson remained untouched by his fame and did not try to assess his talent. Always unassuming about his work, he asked one purchaser of a horse over two feet tall, "Do you have a little boy? Let him ride it!"

Caego and Hunter. Henry Marques. Painted cement. Dog: 18½″ x 15½″.
Hunter: 27″ x 37″. 1942. Bethlehem, Pa. Courtesy of Barbara Johnson, Esq.
Photograph: Clem Fiori

Caego with his shining row of teeth seems eager to accompany his master
on the hunt. An example of folk art in which the relationship of the animal
and man is integral to the art.

Leopard Sculpture
Elijah Pierce (b. 1892)
Carved and painted wood
11″ x 6″
1978
Columbus, Ohio
Courtesy of Bert Hemphill
Photograph: Edward Shoffstall

One of a series for a zoo made in 1920 by Elijah Pierce, who decided to surprise his wife with a carved elephant for her birthday. She was so enthralled that he has carved many animals since then.

Wood Carving

THROUGHOUT THE COUNTRY men continued to find enjoyment in carving menageries of animals in the twentieth century. Many of these sculptors honed their carving skills in jobs that involved woodworking, such as carpentry and lumberjacking. Woodsmen who acquired a love for animals quite naturally made them subjects of their art. Some artists did not begin to carve until retirement; others used carving as a relief from tedious jobs and harsh reality. All found solace in their animals and the "environments" they created much in the same manner that some women lose themselves in their dollhouses.

Penguin Tenpins
Anonymous
Painted wood
12″ height
Early 20th century
Eastern seaboard
Courtesy of Lillian and
Jerry Grossman

Part of a set of bowling pins.

Ram Sculpture. Anonymous. Carved and painted wood with applied ram's
horns and leather ears. 18″ height. Early 20th century. New England.
Courtesy of Aarne Anton, New York City. Photograph: Steven Tucker

A tender portrait in wood of a ram's head. Striving for a naturalistic effect,
the artist used real ram's horns.

Baboon. Anonymous. Carved and painted wood. 13″ x 13″ x 11″. c. 1910.
Courtesy of Allan Katz

This carving might have been part of a carnival ring-toss game. While the
head displays an academic style of carving, the body and arms reflect the
whimsey of the artist.

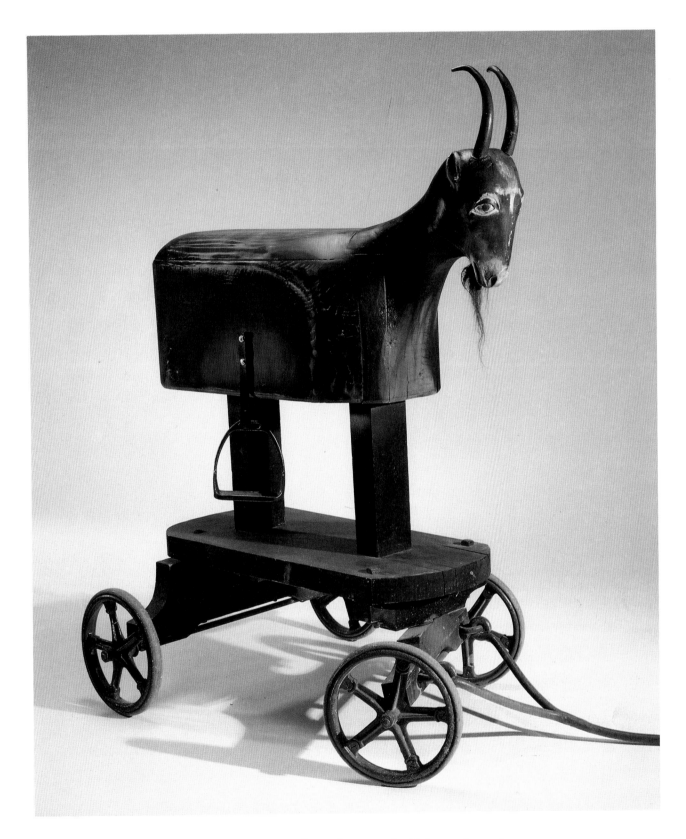

Goat Initiation Piece. Signed "Sparks". Wood with bronze horns, iron wheels, and horsehair goatee. 47″ x 34″. Dated Jan. 30, 1926. Courtesy of Walowen & Schneider. Photograph: Edwin Shoffstall

Designed for a fraternity initiation rite.

Rocking Horse. Philadelphia Toboggan Company Carvers. Carved and painted wood. 47″ x 35″ x 14″. c. 1906. Philadelphia. Courtesy of Charlotte Dinger. Photograph: Bill Kane

This rocking horse, one of three, was made for the children of the owners of the Philadelphia Toboggan Company and one of the carvers. The horse converted to a pulltoy with wooden wheels replacing the rockers.

Horse
Anonymous
Tin
28¼″ x 19½″
1910
Maine
Courtesy of
Barbara Johnson, Esq.
Photograph: Clem Fiori

Stallions
Anonymous
Painted wood
White horse: 11″ x 6¼″
Black horse: 8¾″ x 4¼″
1930s
Connecticut
Courtesy of
Barbara Johnson, Esq.
Photograph: Clem Fiori

Frog and Toad in a Boat
Oscar Peterson (1887–1951)
Carved and painted wood
with glass eyes
14½″ x 3½″ x 4½″
Early 20th century
Cadillac, Mich.
Courtesy of Ronald J. Fritz

Oscar Peterson's work
captured the essence of
northern Michigan wildlife.
He worked mainly on fish
decoys and sculptures, and
created over sixty colorful
plaques, which he sold to bait
shops, hardware stores, and
tourists. According to a
family member, this sculpture
was made as a Christmas
present for Oscar's brother
George, and was based on a
cartoon character.

Nesting Bird
Howard Ortman (1894–1976)
Mixed woods
2½″ x 6″ x 4″
1966
San Francisco
Courtesy of the Ames Gallery
of American Folk Art,
Berkeley, Calif.

The smooth contours of the
bird are also reflected in the
polished twigs, which have
been interwoven with as
much care as a real bird
would employ in building
her nest.

Peacock Plaque
Oscar Peterson (1887–1951)
Carved and painted wood
with glass eyes
23½″ x 10″
1925–1934
Cadillac, Mich.
Courtesy of Ronald J. Fritz

Wall Cupboard
Stephen Huneck (b. 1948)
Carved and painted wood
38″ x 14″ x 6″
1980s
St. Johnsbury, Vt.
Courtesy of Stephen Huneck

Stephen Huneck works out
of a renovated 18th-century
farmhouse. In carving his
numerous animals he endows
them with an infectious sense
of humor. Huneck mixes his
own paints and only uses
local basswood ("It is strong,
will last forever, and doesn't
split").

Whirligig. Matteo Radoslovich (1883–1972). Painted wood and metal. 7¼″ diameter. 20th century. Courtesy of the Museum of American Folk Art

These dogs run faster and faster as the wind blows, chasing each other's tails.

Raccoon
Anonymous
Carved and painted pine
8″ x 5″
c. 1930s
Maine
Private collection
Photograph courtesy of
Kenneth and Ida Manko,
Moody, Maine

This pine raccoon was found
with several other animals at
a flea market in Maine. Rural
whittlers were known to
carve hundreds of animals
over the course of a lifetime,
giving many away as small
gifts and trading others for
services and staples.

Bear on a Log
Anonymous
Various woods
15″ x 8″
Early 20th century
Maine
Courtesy of
Kenneth and Ida Manko,
Moody, Maine

Found in a hunting camp,
this simple yet fine carving
was made by a man with
considerable woodworking
skills. Animals posed on
logs represent an important
genre of the American
woodworking tradition.

Dog Sculpture. Pucho Odio (b. 1928). Carved and painted wood. 48″ x 22″.
1970s. New York City. Courtesy of the Jay Johnson Gallery, New York City

Pucho Odio begins his animals by drawing them on the wood itself, and
then carving with a knife.

Caged Animals. Fred Alten (1872–1945). Animals: carved and painted wood;
cage: wood with metal bars. Cage: 30″ x 12″ x 10″. Early 20th century.
Wyandotte, Mich. Courtesy of Joseph and Lee Dumas

When Joseph and Lee Dumas discovered Alten's animals in a woodshed,
they were astounded to find them "encaged" so securely that to free them
required the use of a small crowbar.

Hippopotamus Sculpture
Fred Alten (1872–1945)
Carved and painted wood
with glass eyes
14″ x 7″
Early 20th century
Wyandotte, Mich.
Courtesy of
Joseph and Lee Dumas

Alten's work as a machinist
helped him achieve sturdy,
correctly balanced sculptures.
Here the legs of the hippopotamus are mortised into
the body, while the head and
neck are mortised in a
complicated steplike section.

FRED ALTEN (1872–1945)

One such man was Fred Alten of Wyandotte, Michigan. Alten, born of German parents in Ohio, moved in 1912 to Wyandotte, where he pursued a variety of menial jobs. He was said to be an introverted man who spent his spare hours in his woodshed carving animals. There he pored over a well-thumbed copy of an 1880 edition of *Johnson's Book of Nature*, which contained illustrations by nineteenth-century naturalists of animals, then set himself to carving every animal pictured in the "encyclopedia." *Johnson's Book of Nature* was dedicated "to the Youth of America who look up from Nature's work to Nature's God and see in all creatures the ministers of Infinite Wisdom"—a sentiment reminiscent of the message in the *Scripture Animals* of Jonathan Fisher. While Alten's religious views remained private, his reverence for the animal kingdom is evident.

Alten's animals also reflect his time spent working in a foundry. Many of his bigger sculptures are joined together in parts rather than carved from a single piece. Some have metal feet and are weighted with inset metal. To achieve a natural appearance Alten painted his animals in their true colors, and sought interesting textures by "combing" furry species after dipping them in wax.

Fred Alten has been compared to Wilhelm Schimmel, who also preferred the company of his animal carvings to the real world of men and women.[16] After finishing a number of animals, Alten would fix them to the floors of wooden cages with metal bars, where they would remain incarcerated for life. Whether they were being "protected" from man or were symbols of a prisoner mentality is anybody's guess. As a final curiosity, even though Alten left a detailed will, he made no provision for the disposal of his beloved menagerie, leaving the carvings untended in a garage, where they were discovered thirty years later.

Lion Sculpture
Fred Alten (1872–1945)
Carved and painted wood
with glass eyes
16½″ x 9¾″
Early 20th century
Wyandotte, Mich.
Courtesy of
Joseph and Lee Dumas

Alten's lion is one of his most expressive works, combining an impressionistic head with a sleek body. The legs are mortised into the body.

Cat Sculpture
Fred Alten (1872–1945)
Carved and painted wood
11″ x 3½″
Early 20th century
Wyandotte, Mich.
Courtesy of
Joseph and Lee Dumas

The cat is carved from one piece of wood. Underneath the paint there is a layer of combed wax, creating a hairy texture.

Turkey Sculpture
Miles Carpenter (1889–1985)
Painted and carved wood
12″ x 7″
1974
Waverly, Va.
Courtesy of Bert Hemphill
Photograph: Edward Shoffstall

Miles Carpenter "saw" animals in the stumps and limbs in his woodpile. "I can see things in them. If it's something I like, I'll keep it. If not, I'll throw it away." His porch and kitchen were filled with animals of every variety—a kangaroo with a baby in its pouch, a snapping turtle, a turkey, a squirrel climbing a tree, and a monkey with babies hanging from its tail.

MILES CARPENTER (1889–1985)

"There's an old story about wood, and it's true. The story is that there's something in there, under the surface of every piece of wood. You don't need no design 'cause it's right there; you just take the bark off and if you do it good you can find something."
—Miles Carpenter[7]

Although Miles Carpenter's fame rests on a larger body of work than animals, he carved a substantial number of creatures, painting them in bright, primary colors. While some sculptures appear realistic, others grew out of the wood he selected, the shapes directed by roots and branches. "I started making things out of roots because I seen something funny in them. I would look at roots from a tree that fell down, or I'd pull some up, and I'd look at all those long and short and thick and thin and tangled parts, and I'd just begin to see something funny . . . . You have to be able to see something in a root—then you just fix it right."[18]

Using chisels, pocketknives, saws, and axes, Carpenter applied his considerable talents to a veritable menagerie, from leaping frogs to sophisticated greyhounds to twenty-foot snakes. When he worked on a block of wood, he would draw a pattern of the animal on a piece of paper, cut it out, and lay it over the wood. From his early days as a carver in 1940, he made it a practice to save the pattern for future use.

Carpenter spent most of his life enjoying the quiet, small-town ambiance of Waverly, Virginia. In 1940, finding his lumber business dull, he started carving animals, but quit a couple of years later until his retirement in 1957. He was devastated by his wife's death in 1966, and found solace in carving, often including in his sculptures bits of fur and other accessories that had belonged to her.

Discovered in the early 1970s, Carpenter soon achieved worldwide fame. He delighted in showing people his sculpture and loved to see their reactions. Once a woman brought him a piece of driftwood, doubting that he could find anything in it. Now there is an animal in each knob: an alligator, a dirty rat, a fish, and, last but not least, Mickey Mouse![19]

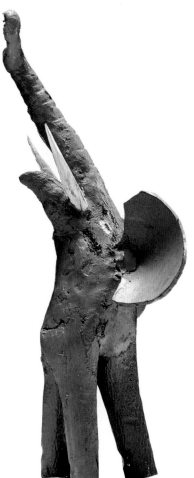

Elephant Sculpture
Miles Carpenter (1889–1985)
Painted and carved wood
10″ height
1982
Waverly, Va.
Courtesy of Bert Hemphill
Photograph: Edward Shoffstall

Kentucky Carvers

IN THE BACKWOODS of Kentucky, Tennessee, and North Carolina, life held few changes in the early twentieth century. Men from a whittling tradition found carving one of the few pleasures they could afford. Appalachian sculpture reflected the isolation and independence of mountain life: many carvers focused on religious subjects, the people themselves, and the animals around them.

Tiger Sculpture
Minnie and Garland Adkins
(Minnie b. 1934,
Garland b. 1928)
Carved and painted wood
34½″ x 9″
1988
Eastern Kentucky
Courtesy of the Kentucky
Art and Craft Foundation,
Louisville, Ky.

Mother Pig and Piglets. Minnie and Garland Adkins (Minnie b. 1934,
Garland b. 1928). Acrylic on basswood. Mother pig: 28″ x 14″. 1988.
Eastern Kentucky. Courtesy of the Kentucky Art and Craft Foundation,
Louisville, Ky.

The Adkins house is filled with wooden critters in various stages of
construction. All appendages are carved or whittled out rather than glued
onto the bodies. Garland Adkins usually roughs out the larger animals while
his wife finishes the pieces and paints them.

Mother Possum and Babies. Minnie and Garland Adkins
(Minnie b. 1934, Garland b. 1928). Carved and painted wood.
25″ x 8″. 1988. Eastern Kentucky. Courtesy of the Kentucky
Art and Craft Foundation, Louisville, Ky.

One of the more aggressive works by the Adkinses, the Mother
Possum's fierce set of teeth contrast with the apparent
helplessness of her young.

Mud Puppy
Anonymous
Carved and painted wood
4¾″ x 13″
c. 1900
Randolph County, N.C.
Courtesy of
Tony and Marie Shank
Photograph:
Ted Whisnant

Years ago small mud puppies
(salamanders) were used by
fishermen to "jigger" fish
(done by slapping the hooked
bait on top of the water to
attract fish to strike). This
rare carving was prob-
ably made by a fisherman
who caught "the big ones"
with help from his mud
puppies.

Frog Creature
Minnie Black (b. 1899)
Gourds, papier-mâché, paint,
and shellac
12″ x 6″ x 4″
1988
Laurel County, Ky.
Courtesy of Larry Hackley
and the Kentucky Art and
Craft Foundation,
Louisville, Ky.

Minnie Black grows
thousands of gourds that she
turns into sculptures. While
her sense of humor is evident
in all of her work, sculptures
range from the timid to the
aggressive and grotesque. Her
animals are both real and '
imagined.

Cat Sculpture
Linvel Barker (b. 1929)
Painted wood
12″ x 10″
1988
East Kentucky
Courtesy of Larry Hackley
and the Kentucky Art and
Craft Foundation,
Louisville, Ky.

Linvel Barker, a retired steel-
mill worker, began carving
his sleek animals about 1986,
using wood cut on his
property. His wife, Faye,
paints the eyes.

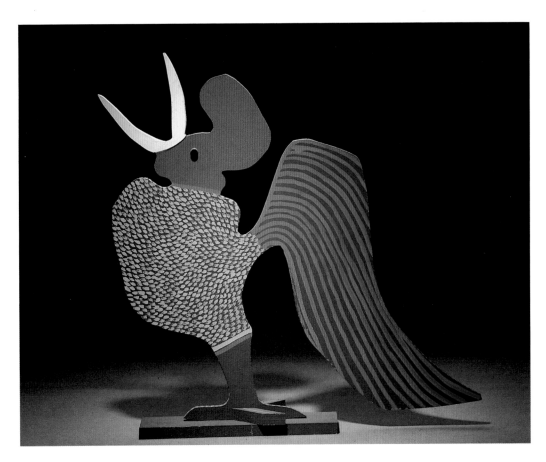

Crowing Rooster
Marvin Finn (b. 1918)
Carved and painted wood
24½″ x 25″
1988
Louisville, Ky.
Courtesy of the Kentucky
Art and Craft Foundation,
Louisville, Ky.

Although Finn calls his work "whittling," he uses a band saw as well as a knife, and the wood he selects is flat instead of rounded. Finn gets his ideas "from my imagination and from looking at something beautiful every day. You ever look at a chicken? It's got hundreds and hundreds of different colors on him." (Quoted by Dick Kaukas, *The Courier-Journal,* April 11, 1987, p. 5.) Finn likes to cover his animals with hundreds of dots, lines, and circles.

Rooster
Marvin Finn (b. 1918)
Carved and painted wood
25″ x 25″
1988
Louisville, Ky.
Courtesy of the Kentucky
Art and Craft Foundation,
Louisville, Ky.

Marvin Finn was one of twelve children growing up on a farm in Clio, Alabama. His only toys were those he made. Finn held a variety of jobs and didn't work full time on his carvings, toys, and constructions until he retired.

Yellow Snake
Edd Lambdin (b. 1935)
Carved and painted wood
49″ length
1988
East Kentucky
Courtesy of Larry Hackley
and the Kentucky Art and
Craft Foundation,
Louisville, Ky.

Lizard
Edd Lambdin (b. 1935)
Carved and painted wood
40″ length
1988
East Kentucky
Courtesy of Larry Hackley
and the Kentucky Art and
Craft Foundation,
Louisville, Ky.

Edd Lambdin carves animals
exclusively—mostly birds,
monkeys, snakes, lizards, cats,
dogs, and alligator canes
made from roots and limbs
found in the mountains
around his home.

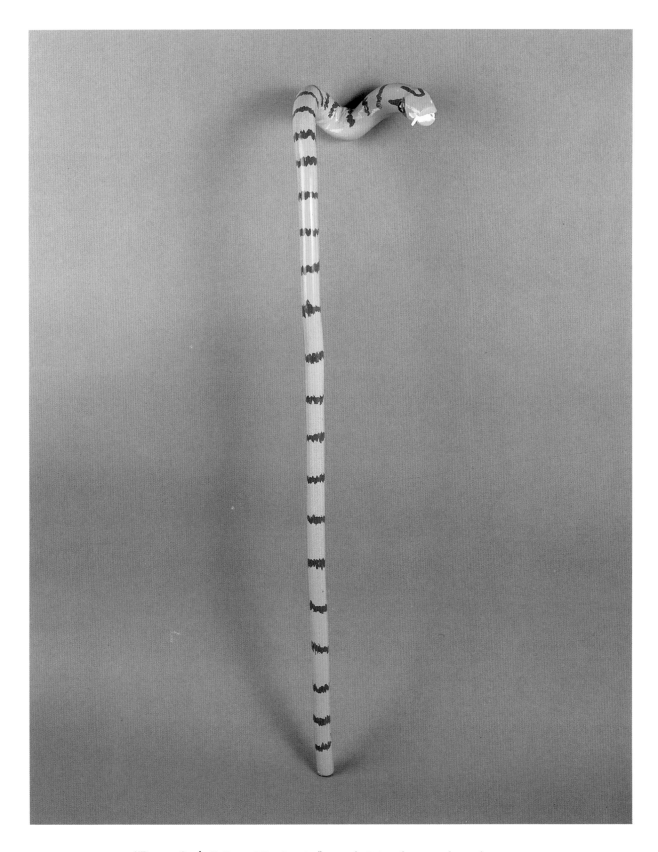

"Brown Snake" Cane. Tim Lewis (b. 1952). Painted root and wood.
40″ length. 1988. Eastern Kentucky. Courtesy of Larry Hackley
and the Kentucky Art and Craft Foundation, Louisville, Ky.

Tim Lewis makes canes from the roots of small trees dug up in the hills
around his home. His carved roots become snakes, lizards, dinosaurs, birds,
dogs, even a space shuttle. He has painted a "habitat" on the cane shaft for
the animal carved on the handle.

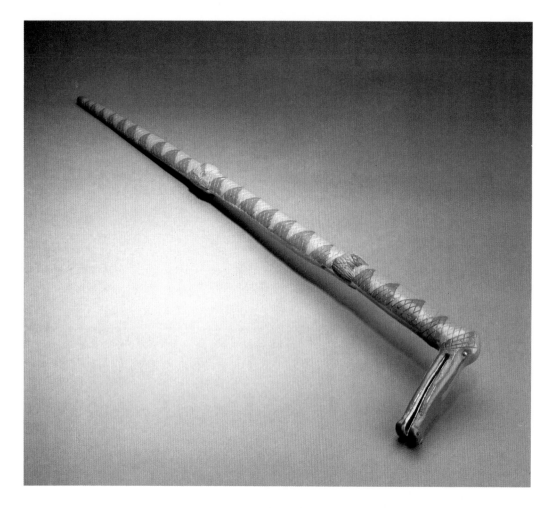

Alligator Cane. Denzil Goodpaster (b. 1908). Carved and painted wood. 39½" length. 1986. Eastern Kentucky. Courtesy of Larry Hackley and the Kentucky Art and Craft Foundation, Louisville, Ky.

Denzil Goodpaster, a retired farmer, began carving canes about 1970 and has recently begun to sculpt. His most famous canes depict such disparate subjects as Dolly Parton, ladies eaten by animals, and ladies with snakes wrapped around them.

Cane with Two Entwined Snakes. Larry McKee (b. 1941). Paint and shellac on cedar. 41½" length. 1988. Eastern Kentucky. Courtesy of Larry Hackley and the Kentucky Art and Craft Foundation, Louisville, Ky.

Using cedar found in the woods around his home, Larry McKee makes canes of snakes, sometimes embellishing them with other animals, people, and skeletons.

Giraffe
Edgar Tolson (1904–1984)
Carved poplar
11¼″ x 9½″
1971
Compton, Ky.
Courtesy of the
Hall Collection
of American Folk Art
Photograph: Michael Hall

EDGAR TOLSON (1904–1984)

Edgar Tolson of Compton, Kentucky, is almost a stereotype of a Kentucky mountainman, an itinerant worker who has been by turns preacher, farmer, and chairmaker. Throughout his somewhat checkered career marked by bouts with the bottle, Tolson continued carving. Like many other folk artists, Tolson became more serious about his art after a prolonged illness. He suffered a stroke in 1957 and was forced to give up construction work and carpentry. To replace needed lost income, he began carving snake canes and animals that he either traded or sold for small sums. In 1967 his fortune changed for the better when he was "discovered" at a crafts fair. Today he is Kentucky's most famous carver.

Although many of Tolson's sculptures are vignettes of biblical scenes or portraits of mountain life, a number of them contain animals. These animals express Tolson's skill with the knife, as well as reveal his deep feelings for them.

Horse
Edgar Tolson (1904–1984)
Carved and painted wood
13¼″ x 10″
1971
Compton, Ky.
Courtesy of the
Hall Collection
of American Folk Art
Photograph: Michael Hall

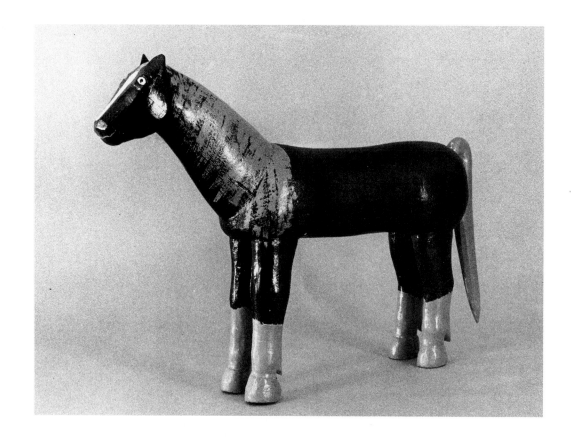

Kangaroo
Edgar Tolson (1904–1984)
Carved poplar
6″ x 1¾″
1970
Compton, Ky.
Courtesy of the
Hall Collection
of American Folk Art
Photograph: Michael Hall

Wildcat Candlestick
Edgar Alexander McKillop
(1879–1950)
Carved walnut with bone
teeth and glass eyes
Wildcat: 5″ x 6½″
Candlestick: 9″ height
c. 1930s
Balfour, N.C.
Courtesy of
Tony and Marie Shank
Photograph: Ted Whisnant

EDGAR ALEXANDER MCKILLOP (1878–1950)

Edgar Alexander McKillop was born in the farming community of Balfour, North Carolina, into a family of people who made almost everything they needed. As he grew older he moved around quite a lot in search of work, finally quitting for good around 1924. After being given a gift of wood, he feverishly began to carve, working full time at his "occupation." A neighbor recalled, "He was always hewing on an animal. . . . That's all he done all day long."[20] As in the case of Fred Alten, McKillop's background as a machinist, logger, and general handyman provided him with the necessary skills to create large pieces with complicated constructions. Like Jesse Aaron (see p. 201), McKillop sometimes finished his works with a "burning iron," searing rather than carving the feathers of his eagles.[21]

Unlike some of his fellow carvers who worked in secrecy, McKillop enjoyed showing off his menagerie, which he kept in his house even though it threatened to take over the family's living quarters. During the Depression he customized a pickup truck to hold the animals, carting them to neighboring towns where he would charge viewers a small admission to the show. In the late 1930s McKillop parted with a number of his beloved animals in order to buy a small farm for his family.

McKillop filled his modest millhouse with a handmade menagerie. He acquired wood from three or four black walnut trees and devoted himself to his sculpture. His daughter Lelia said of him, "And he never done any carving until he just got that wood. . . . It was just in him—just talented." The Abby Aldrich Rockefeller Folk Art Center was one of the first museums to recognize his genius.

"Standing Bear"
Edgar Alexander McKillop
(1879–1950)
Walnut with painted rodent's
teeth and button eyes
21½″ x 8″
c. 1930s
Balfour, N.C.
Courtesy of the Ackland Art
Museum, The University of
North Carolina at Chapel
Hill, Ackland Fund

McKillop's rendition of his
"Standing Bear" can be
compared to bear carvings by
the Northwest Coast Indians
—note the bear's dignity, and
the inclusion of rodent teeth.

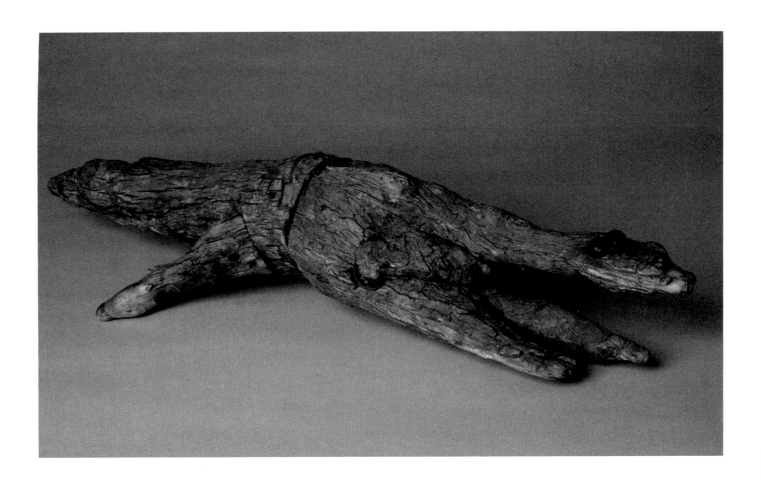

JESSE AARON (1887–1979)

Jesse Aaron, an artist who did not start carving until he was in his seventies, began by scavenging pieces of wood that suggested the shapes of various animals. He then used chain saws, knives, chisels, and drills to bring out the animal that he believed was already in the wood itself, declaring, "God put the faces in the wood."[22] Aaron not only worked with found wood (mostly cedar or cypress) but also applied found objects for special effects. Some pieces were seared with a hot iron to form interesting textures.

Aaron's anthropomorphic visions can be partly attributed to a religious fervor frequently encountered in poverty-stricken rural areas A descendant of many cross-cultural traditions from his Seminole, white/black ancestry, Aaron distilled powerful animal images from a diverse body of folklore.

Today many contemporary carvers, including Ralph Griffin and John Abdul-jaami, are creating impressionistic animals from found pieces of wood. Each represents a highly personal statement that reflects the eye of the creator.

Animal
Jesse Aaron (1887–1979)
Carved wood and beads
Dimensions unavailable
1970s
Gainesville, Fla.
Courtesy of the Janet Fleisher Gallery, Philadelphia

Aaron selected his wood, usually cedar or cypress, and cut and hauled it home despite the fact that he was over seventy when he started to sculpt. Aaron would never make a piece that wasn't his own idea and he let the wood itself direct his carving.

Totem. Jesse Aaron (1887–1979). Carved wood and beads. 42″ x 21″ x 17″.
1970s. Gainesville, Fla. Courtesy of the Cavin-Morris Gallery, New
York City

Jesse Aaron believed that spirits inhabited the logs he chose for his work.

Coyote
Felipe Benito Archuleta
(b. 1910)
Carved and painted
cottonwood with teeth,
marble eyes, and sisal
whiskers
35½″ x 56″ x 9½″
1982
Santa Fe, N.M.
Courtesy of the Museum of
American Folk Art

Felipe Archuleta has been
called the heir to a rich
Spanish heritage of carved
and painted wood. He marks
the transition from the
traditional New Mexican
woodworker to the
contemporary sculptor.

The Southwest Carving Tradition

THE SOUTHWEST is the home of a group of contemporary sculptors whose
Hispanic heritage of religious carvings burst forth into a new idiom in the 1970s.
Stemming from the gaily decorated altars, brightly colored statues of saints, and
appealing crèche figures of the eighteenth and nineteenth centuries, a menagerie
of carved animals appeared on the New Mexico scene. Like Kachina dolls, the
dolls made by neighboring Hopi and Zuni Indians, most were carved from cottonwood. The father of this lively "school" is Felipe Archuleta (b. 1910), a crusty
iconoclast, whose expressive animal sculpture enjoys worldwide acclaim.

Born and raised in New Mexico, Archuleta grew up surrounded by religious
icons made by local Hispanic craftsmen. A lifetime of itinerant jobs and unrelent-
ing poverty appeared to be Archuleta's lot. In 1939 while working as a WPA
watchman, he sold his first carving to a shopkeeper for $1.75. This sale represented
the germination of his career, even though it would be another eighteen years
before Archuleta seriously began carving. During that time he worked as a carpenter, until one day he suddenly quit, looking for an outlet for his long-suppressed
creativity: "One time I was bringing my groceries and I ask God for some kind of

miracle, some kind of thing to do, to give me something to make my life with . . . some kind of a thing I can make. So I started for about three days, I started carving after that. And they just come out of my mind after that."²³

At first Archuleta experimented with a variety of carvings, including twirlies and small animals. By the 1970s, perhaps at the urging of the Santa Fe galleries, a body of lifesize animal sculptures emerged. Archuleta carved like a man possessed. As if to make up for lost time, he created a menagerie that could have graced Noah's Ark: fierce-looking lions with shaggy manes and sharp teeth, wooly sheep covered with fragments of uncarded fleece, and howling coyotes destined to become an overused symbol of the Southwestern school of animal sculpture. For the first time in his life, Archuleta took pride in his work, poring over children's animal books for inspiration and guidance. His perfectionism extended to his choice of materials, from the carefully selected stumps of cottonwood to the imaginative use of broom bristles, marbles, and other found objects for claws, teeth, ears, and eyes.

Archuleta's not-so-tame animals display a belligerency frequently expressed by a mouthful of ferocious teeth (he achieves this effect by implanting jagged white

Giraffe Sculpture
Felipe Benito Archuleta
(b. 1910)
Carved and painted wood,
plastic pine bough
25″ height, 22″ base
1975
Santa Fe, N.M.
Courtesy of Bert Hemphill
Photograph:
Edward Shoffstall

teeth in the sculpted dark snouts). At times some of his animals have wistful expressions; always they resonate with human traits.

The Hispanic tradition of the workshop and apprentice system led Archuleta to hire a number of local men (including his son) to collaborate on his animals. He thereby instituted an informal school of southwestern carvers who were alternately inspired by his genius and enraged by his temperamental outbursts. Alonzo Jimenez, David Alvarez, and Leroy Archuleta eventually left his employ to strike out on their own. They in turn are now influencing their disciples and a number of independent craftsmen who have been inspired by the success of their animals. While some of the work of Archuleta's successors has been mediocre, the best of the New Mexican carvers merit attention. However, most observers concur that Archuleta is in a class by himself—a true innovator who left his mark for others to follow.

Alligator
Alonzo Jimenez
Carved and painted wood
42″ x 4½″
1980s
New Mexico
Courtesy of the
Elaine Horwitch Gallery,
Santa Fe, N.M.

The popularity of Alonzo Jimenez's animals worries him—he does not like to make two of anything. Working with cottonwood found on his own land in Chupadero, Jimenez creates large animals. Although he started out working for Felipe Archuleta, he now has a strong following of his own.

Armadillo
David Alvarez (b. 1953)
Painted cottonwood
8″ x 19″ x 7″
1984
Santa Fe, N.M.
Courtesy of the Museum of
American Folk Art

David Alvarez has emerged from the "Archuleta school" of wood carving to create a softer, less aggressive body of animals than those favored by Archuleta.

Deer Drawing. Martin Ramirez (c. 1885–1960). Colored pencil on paper.
17½″ x 24″. c. 1953. Auburn, Calif. Courtesy of the Janet Fleisher Gallery,
Philadelphia

Ramirez frequently chose the deer as a central theme, playing on feelings of
helplessness and fear. His deer appear trapped and reflect man's violence
toward his fellow creatures.

Horse and Rider
Martin Ramirez
(c. 1885–1960)
Pencil on paper
24″ x 25″
1950s
California
Private collection
Photograph courtesy of the
Phylis Kind Galleries,
Chicago and New York City

Looking like a Mexican
bandito, the rider aims his
gun in a pose typical of
Ramirez's work.

MARTIN RAMIREZ (c. 1885–1960)

In California the Hispanic tradition in folk art animals is represented by Martin Ramirez, who for many years suffered as a mute and withdrawn psychotic, finding his only means of expression through his art. Ramirez's controlled images, frequently focusing on animals, are famous for their hypnotic sense of space and pattern. Perhaps unconsciously drawing upon a variety of styles and ideas present in his Mexican American heritage, Ramirez created animals in a formal framework that utilized intricate designs.

As a young man, Ramirez emigrated from Mexico and held a number of menial jobs, including working on the railroad. Around 1915 he lost the ability to cope and stopped speaking entirely. In 1930 he was picked up as a vagrant in California and institutionalized as a schizophrenic for the rest of his life. His achievement is all the more extraordinary when one considers his working conditions and supplies. Not only did he depend upon the meager provisions of the ward, but until his doctor intervened, his drawings were thrown away by the staff as a matter of policy. Dr. Tarno Pasto wrote in 1954:

> His manner of work is unique. When good paper is not available, he glues together
> scraps of paper, old envelopes, paper bags, paper cups, wrappers—anything that may

have a clear drawing area. He often makes many small background studies, seashell and nature forms, which he stores in his shirt, in a paper shopping bag, in tied rolls, or behind a radiator, suddenly to be taken out and glued to an evolving picture. He fashions his own glue out of mashed potatoes and water—sometimes bread and saliva. He squats on his haunches, moving about the floor between two cots, using stubs of colored pencils and Crayolas, drawing a little here, a little there. His drawing is kept rolled up and usually only a portion of it is exposed at any one time.[24]

The animals of Ramirez—frightened-looking deer, boars, horses, tigers, and prairie dogs—reinforce the feeling of entrapment in his pictures. A deer in a space that appears too small for it is pressed in by enclosing walls, or a tiger gazes uncertainly into a tunnel without end. The image of a horse and rider apparently held special meaning for Ramirez, for he repeated it often. His riders look like Mexican cowboys or bandits, burdened with shoulder harnesses holding reams of bullets. The horses' heads are thrown back—they appear taut with tension, ready to rear at the slightest provocation.

Tiger Drawing
Martin Ramirez
(c. 1885–1960)
Pencil and crayon
Approximately 24″ square
1950s
California
Private collection
Photograph courtesy of the
Phylis Kind Galleries,
Chicago and New York City

An anxious tiger peers into a cave or tunnel looking to hide or find safety—a theme that Ramirez worked on again and again.

Midwestern Animal Folk Potters

WHILE MOST of the twentieth-century artists in this book have been described
in terms of their biographies, talents, and motives, one group of folk artists remains
individually anonymous. It is perhaps fitting that they conclude the procession of
animaliers, for not only do they remind us of the past, but they also focused on the
symbol of the animal kingdom, the royal lion or King of Beasts.

Emerging from a heritage of traditional eighteenth- and nineteenth-century
earthenware and stoneware pottery, a new form of animal folk sculpture appeared
in the early twentieth century, made by men working in the sewer and tile potteries in Michigan and Ohio. Workers created these end-of-the-day pieces for
themselves, to give as presents or sell for extra income. They modeled the leftover
moist clay that if not used would have hardened into unusable lumps. Townspeople were willing to pay up to fifty cents for the glazed animal figures they often
used as decorative doorstops.[25] Although a number of species were represented,
including turtles and frogs, the most common form was the lion. In Grand Ledge,

Michigan, so many were made that people began to speak of the "Grand Ledge lion" as a distinct category. Although Grand Ledge lions were molded, they manage to be individually expressive; some smile, some appear regal, and others are clownish with their tongues lolling from the sides of their mouths.

As people discovered sewer-tile sculpture, the stoneware potteries themselves began using molds to re-create the most popular items such as the lion on a base. However, most forms remained limited to sewer-tile plants, with workers teaching their fellow workers, handing down "recipes" from the time the first lion was made (probably about 1900) until well into the 1940s. One worker, Harry Poole, explained the process:

> Just before noon some fellows would take some clay and pack the molds tightly. A lot of the molds were not filled properly and the lions never came out right. We would then set the mold aside until the next day when we would take the lion out of the mold and smooth it all out by licking your thumb. Some guys put tongues in their

Sewer-Tile Lion
Anonymous
Sewer tile
17″ x 32″
c. 1870
Ohio
Courtesy of
Hirschl & Adler Folk,
New York City

The lion, a favorite subject for end-of-the-day pieces, was made from a plaster-of-Paris mold and was baked in the same kiln as production pieces.

lions by using a knife to make the mouth open and then rolling some molding clay. The paws, tail and mane were fixed by using a knife or pencil. Then the lion was placed on a sand-covered board and put in the kiln with the tile.[26]

Men who spent their free time at the kiln loved their animals indeed, for the making of them broke the monotony of the average day. An anonymous worker inadvertently told the story of animals in American folk art when he said, "Rarely a week went by without somethin' bein' made."[27]

Dog-Faced Pottery Pitcher
Anonymous
Salt-glazed brown clay
10¼″ x 7″
Late 19th century
Midwest
Courtesy of
Edward L. Steckler

Factory workers confronted by leftover, moist clay at the end of a day's work made figural items for their own amusement. Although this type of pottery was introduced in the 19th century, it was made well into the 20th century.

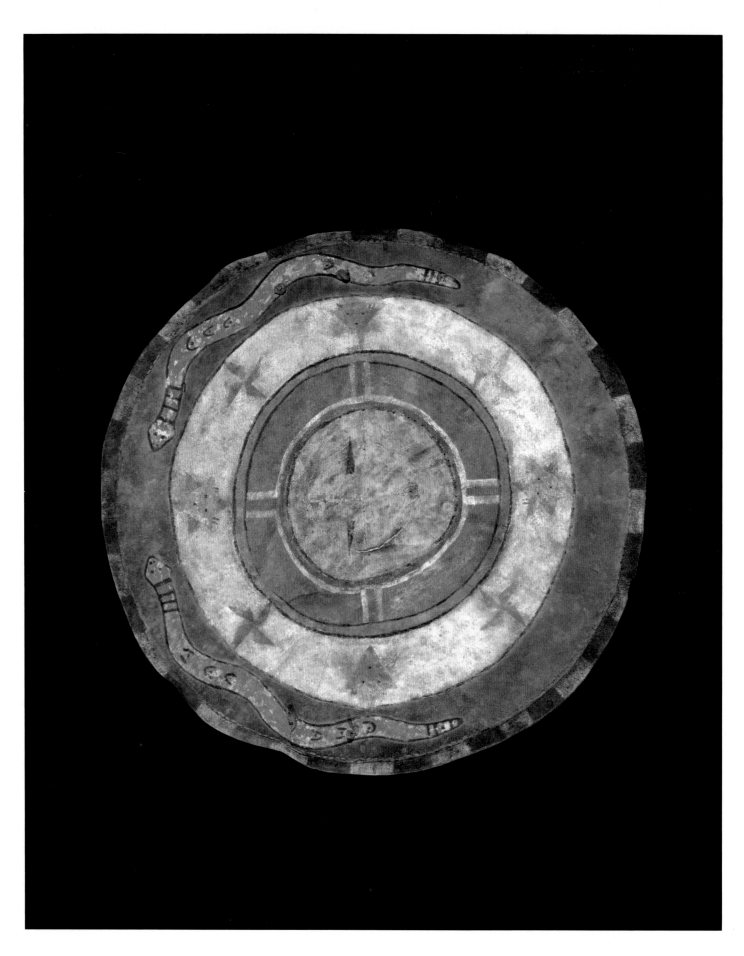

ANIMALS IN
NATIVE AMERICAN
ART

IN THE INDIAN world animals were part of a spiritual pantheon and were thus depicted with a reverence not generally seen in "European" art. A mystical interpretation of animals emphasized the essence of power as well as beauty. Although the many tribes had differing views of the world, they all believed animals were as important as themselves. In one sense animals were considered superior to human beings in that animals possessed sacred powers, which men tried to acquire. Not surprisingly, the animal painted on a shield or carved into a ceremonial pipe is very different from the same creature when depicted on a vase or a painting in the European tradition.

The impressive diversity found in Native American art stems from varied tribal responses to dissimilar environments spread over a vast land. While all Native Americans were descendants of a basic Stone Age culture, various groups developed their own traditions. In the Southwest at the beginning of the Christian era there were three separate flourishing groups: the Anasazi, who inhabited parts of Colorado, Utah, Arizona, and New Mexico; the Hohokam of southern Arizona; and the Magollon of southwestern New Mexico. Each developed its own designs and patterns of decoration. The Mimbres created outstanding images on pottery for six hundred years (A.D. 550–1150) and are famous for their animal and human figures. Ceremonial bowls featuring the animals that were part of their lives (rabbits, birds, fish, deer, bugs, and rodents) were painted (probably by women using yucca brushes).[1] These stylized animals, partly composed of detailed geometric

OPPOSITE PAGE:
Acoma Shield
Acoma Pueblo
Mineral pigments on rawhide
21″ diameter
c. 1850
New Mexico
Private collection
Photograph courtesy of
Joshua Baer & Company,
Santa Fe, N.M.

Most of the Pueblo tribes in the Southwest associate snakes with lightning. Since lightning portends rain and rain signifies germination and growth of corn, snakes are intricately tied to the life cycle.

designs, have been compared to the most sophisticated animals found in modern art. How these techniques developed is still to be discovered. The period of greatest artistic development of representational Mimbres pottery was short-lived. By 1100 the collapse of the Mimbres culture was indicated by the disappearance of its painted ware, and it wasn't until 1600 that the Apaches occupied the valley that once was home to the Mimbres people.

The neighboring Hohokam and Anasazi decorated some of their pottery with animal forms, particularly birds. In extolling the spontaneity of Hohokam pottery, Charles Avery Amsden, a southwestern historian, noted: "Flying birds are evoked with a Z and a horizontal dash, or two down strokes to form a curving V. . . . A dog's ear is cocked with a single cunning blob, his tail set for wagging by a touch of the brush. A bird's leg poised nervously for a forward step . . . a lizard's pointed head—all are rendered with one simple stroke. Best of all are the birds; lanky road runners or fat little quail, they have individuality and life."[2]

Like the Mimbres and other ancient cultures in the area, the Hohokam disappeared sometime after 1100, leaving few traces of their existence save for pottery shards, prehistoric cave paintings, murals, and petroglyphs. Many of these "documents" feature animals of the area, from mountain sheep to snakes. Kiva paintings, spanning the transition from ancient to historic times, provide information about the daily lives of southwestern Indians and the animals among them. Although Kiva painting originated in prehistoric times, a flowering of the art depicting birds, reptiles, and animal forms occurred during the transitional period. One important excavation revealed a kiva (a ceremonial subterranean chamber) in the ancient pueblo of Kuaua in what is now New Mexico. Animals depicted include buffalo, rabbits, fish, birds, and snakes. It wasn't until the nineteenth century that the world began to hear about the remarkable prehistoric paintings in the Southwest. It fell to army officers and surveyors, often the first non-Indians in a sacred kiva, to report and occasionally reproduce some of the wall paintings. As late as the end of the nineteenth century, documents cite Hopi murals portraying hunters and animals. In 1881 a visitor to Jemez described a kiva mural containing pictures of "turkeys, two eagles fighting, hares . . . deer . . . Indians shooting turkeys (with bows and arrows)—the turkeys on a tree. Deer suckling fawn. Buffalo, Mountain Lion springing upon a Buffalo. An eagle grasping a fawn in its talons . . . another turkey . . . a duck, and Eagle chasing ducks."[3]

Watercolor of a Pictograph
Forrest Kirkland
8⅞" x 14⅛"
Dated July 24, 1935
Meyer Springs, Tex.
Courtesy of the
Texas Memorial Museum,
Acc. #2261–73

The abundance of game animals in early times is clearly revealed by this copy of a pictograph. The original rock art dates from A.D. 600–1000.

The developmental significance of Kiva painting, with its panoramic scenes and stylized designs, can be seen throughout the historic period. Ancient cave drawings set the stage for paintings in sacred kivas, on pottery, on hides, and eventually on ledger paper.

The many forms of artistic expression involving animals from the Stone Age to the modern era evolved as responses to spiritual concerns and a desire to ornament and record heroic exploits. While in the West animals decorated prehistoric pottery and painting, in the East animals were more often sculptural figures. Archeologists have found numerous pottery vessels using animal forms in the Mississippi Valley—vessels in the shape of animals or jars decorated with the limbs and the heads of animals. These "sculptors of the east," as they are sometimes called, created a pantheon of animals in stone and wood that were probably intended as funerary offerings.

In Woodlands art spiritual rites were conceived to maintain a balance between opposing natural forces. Winged serpents, symbols of cosmological unity, appeared as intermediaries whose function was to bring together the conflicting elements of the sky and underworld. These winged serpents were composed of parts of celestial birds and underworld serpents. Numerous examples of bird and serpent imagery suggest that a system of metaphoric references evolved into cosmological and artistic conventions in Woodlands art at a very early date.[4]

Although celestial birds and underwater monsters were primary symbols, Woodlands Indians considered animals of every ilk to be spirit emissaries. Even though the Woodlands tribes depended on an agricultural economy, they also hunted, and felt a kinship with the animal kingdom. Eastern Woodlands tribes fashioned ceremonial masks of a variety of animals that expressed both reverence and fear. A Winnebago medicine man expounded on his integral oneness with the spirits who inhabited the forests, the animals, and man: "I came from above and I am holy. This is my second life on earth. . . . At one time I became transformed into a fish. At another time I became a buffalo. From my buffalo existence I was permitted to go to my higher spirit-home, from which I had originally come."[5]

It was through the medium of sculpture, often defined by the smoking pipe, that the Woodlands and Plains Indians revealed their preoccupation with the animal world. The ritual of pipe smoking is found throughout North American Indian life, emerging during the late Archaic period (1000–250 B.C.). Early Woodlands people carved a variety of animal pipes out of fired-clay tubes and soapstone. Smoking pipes featured animal images as an expression of the religious experience. By smoking these pipes, men hoped to be granted gifts from animal spiritual emissaries, who had the power to impart hunting prowess and skills of healing. A vari-

Southwestern Indian Pot
Acoma Pueblo
Polychromed clay-based
pottery
10½″ x 11½″ x 11″
c. 1890
Courtesy of the Janet Fleisher
Gallery, Philadelphia

Acoma is one of the oldest
pueblos in America. Its
potters frequently painted
deer and birds as well as
flowers and geometric
designs on a variety of pots.

Santo Domingo Bird Pot
Santo Domingo Pueblo
Red clay, cream slip, and
black paint
15¾″ height
c. 1910
Santo Domingo Pueblo,
N.M.
Courtesy of the
Denver Art Museum
Photograph: Lloyd Rule

Although most potters from
the Santo Domingo Pueblo
favored geometric designs,
the creator of this pot painted
a row of highly stylized
birds.

Animals in Native American Art / 217

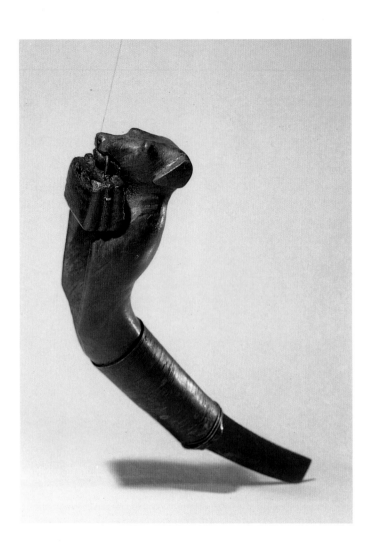

Crooked Knife with
Dog Effigy
Penobscot
Wood and steel
8½″ length
Mid-19th century
Maine
Courtesy of
William E. Channing
Photograph: Peter T. Furst

Before the arrival of the
Europeans, Indians used
knives with blades of sharp,
long beaver teeth. After-
wards, old files, trade knives,
and even straight razors
furnished the steel blades
of the crooked knives.

Bird Ladle
Eastern Woodlands Tribe
Wood
9″ x 5″
Early 19th century
Northeast, probably upstate
New York
Courtesy of
William E. Channing
Photograph: Peter T. Furst

Ladles with bird and other
animal effigies were used by
the Iroquois and their
Algonquian-speaking
neighbors in the ceremonies
and festivals connected with
the harvest of wild berries.

ety of birds, including wrens, ravens, falcons, and cardinals, possessing powers
from the upper world, and a potpourri of animals associated with the underworld
(turtles, snakes, bears, and beavers) predominate in Woodlands sculptures.[6]

Visions prompted the carving of animals on many objects besides pipes—
weapons, bowls, and spoon handles. All were characterized by realistically propor-
tioned animals with simplified facial features and body lines. As early as the 1600s
European travelers commented on the exceptional carving of wooden utensils.
Many of these utensils were fashioned by young men for their brides. As custom
dictated, bridegrooms were expected to provide the household's necessary imple-
ments. While men continued carving as husbands, their most elaborate work was
often fashioned before their marriages. The handle of the crooked knife, an all-
purpose knife, bore intricate carvings of real and mythological animals.

Neighboring Plains tribes shared many cultural and religious ideals with artists
of the Great Lakes tribes and Woodlands tribes and produced similar animal sculptures. On the plains, artists depicted the abundant wildlife native to the interior
continent—the elk, the bighorn sheep, and the awesome grizzly bear. While the

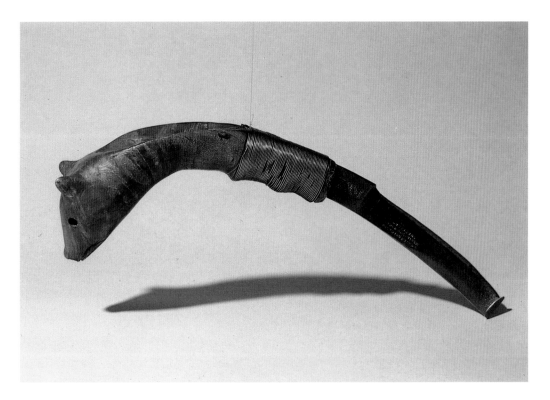

Plains Indians were in awe of the owl's supernatural power, they reserved their greatest admiration for the eagle. Not only did they decorate their shields and war bonnets with eagle feathers, they also carved and painted eagles in prodigious numbers.

However, all of these images pale in frequency and importance when compared to the horse and the buffalo.

The horse, introduced by the Spanish, gave a nomadic people the gift of superior mobility. In turn, the Plains Indians immortalized the horse in song, deed, and art. The horse-dance stick, a specific form of sculpture embodying the horse, had many functions. It was widely carried in ceremonial horse dances to obtain properties of power and healing and it also served to document exploits. One visitor among the Blackfeet, noting the use of the horse-dance stick in various ceremonies, observed "a painted and carved horse used in re-enacting coup by a warrior in the Sun Dance Lodge." He also mentioned that a warrior "who was a noted taker of horses carried a painted horse carved from wood."[7] Men carved horse sticks to honor brave horses killed in battle and, less dramatically, made similar carvings denoting membership in various horse societies.

When Maximilian, Prince of Wied, and his accompanying artist Karl Bodner traveled among the Plains Indians in the 1830s, they discovered that animals played a large role in Plains art, especially in the hide paintings featuring heroic scenes involving stolen or captured horses. Maximilian recorded that he could obtain a painted hide for as little as "5 musket balls and some powder."[8]

The decorating of everyday objects with geometric designs was relegated to women, but the painting of hides, tipi covers, and tipi linings was left to men, who were eager to aggrandize their military accomplishments. Before their exposure to the naturalistic drawings of artists such as Karl Bodner, Indian artists tended to create sticklike figures of men and horses. In 1837 an artist, Alfred Miller, traveling with a caravan of fur traders throughout the West, received a drawing from Ma-wo-ma ("Little Chief"), head of the Snake Indians, probably in return for a portrait Miller painted of the handsome chief. Miller's account of the incident tells how, "In making a drawing for me, such as they send a letter to their friends, he coloured the drawing with a stick; all four legs of the horse were drawn on the same side. His war horse, himself, and his immense helmet of eagle feathers, occupy the whole field, while the enemy are diminutive creatures. . . ."[9]

Horses, buffalo, and other figures in military art were arranged for compositional effect. Unlike traditional nineteenth-century western painters, Indian artists had little use for perspective or realistic color combinations. Parti-colored horses of blue and red or yellow and green parade in striking, stylized fashion across hides of buffalo and elk. Later, when hides were scarce and paper readily obtainable from

Plains Pipe Bowl
Anonymous
Catilinite
10½″ x 4″ x 1″
Late 19th century
Sioux
Minnesota Territories
Courtesy of the
Denver Art Museum
Photograph: Otto Nelson

A sculptural effigy of a running horse. An important part of tribal rituals, the pipe was carved with great care and treated with reverence.

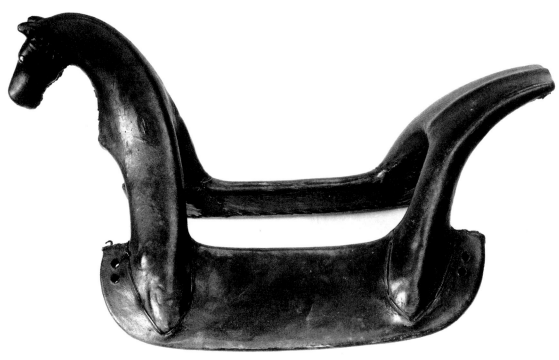

Man's Saddle
Menominee
Tanned hide
Dimensions unavailable
c. 1900
Wisconsin
Courtesy of the American
Museum of Natural History,
Neg. #19699
Photograph: J. Kirschner

This saddle probably honored
a horse for bravery in battle.
It was collected in 1903
somewhere in Wisconsin on
a museum expedition there.

Cree Bark Container
Cree
Birch bark
7½″ height
c. 1900
Manitoba
Courtesy of the Denver Art
Museum

Throughout Alaska and the
subarctic regions, Indian
tribes decorated bark
containers with stylized
geometric motifs and flowing
plant designs. A unique
departure, this storage
container celebrates animals
hunted by the Cree.

Animals in Native American Art / 221

Navajo Horse Pot. Navajo. Clay, orange slip, and paint. 9″ x 6″. Late 19th century. New Mexico and Arizona. Courtesy of the Denver Art Museum. Photograph: Otto Nelson

The Navajos did not have a cultural heritage of decorated pottery, and rarely depicted figures of any kind on their pots. This unique example reflects the importance of the horse in Navajo life.

ledgerbooks, military art, with its rich panoply of horses, buffalo, grizzly bears, elk, and even dogs, appeared on lined sheets of paper with red one-inch margins.

Even during the halcyon days when large buffalo herds thundered over the Great Plains, starvation threatened when game animals were far from camp. To cope, some Indian tribes such as the Plains Ojibwa staged "medicine hunts." "Herb medicines and paint were rubbed on small images or drawings of animals. The supplicant then beat a small hand drum, sang his medicine songs, and prayed for success."[10]

Some warriors believed that the image of a buffalo or grizzly bear, for example, could help protect them from arrows or bullets. The grizzly bear was long admired for its strength and ferocity. Bear petroglyphs inscribed on a sandstone cliff in Nebraska testify to an enduring quest to acquire bear power. The possession of bear power or any other revered animal's spirit was sought to tip the scales in favor of the hunter, and ceremonial fetishes were designed to lure animals back when game was scarce.

While the Plains Indians lived in constant fear of famine, coastal Indians in the Northwest spent their lives fishing and hunting in forests filled with game and seas with fish. Their relative comfort allowed plenty of time for carving a body of

Ceremonial Tipi
Blackfoot
Painted hide
Dimensions unavailable
1892–1894
Western United States
Courtesy of the American
Museum of Natural History,
Neg. #122750

Men of the northern plains painted their ceremonial tipis in a simple, almost pictographic style. Figures and animals appeared in visions, thereby influencing the choice of design. Tipis are part of a legacy of military art depicted on hides and in ledgerbooks.

work that is famous for its sophistication and complexity. Although a carving tradition existed before the Europeans arrived in the eighteenth century, it flourished afterwards. The Europeans introduced new materials, including cloth, buttons, and copper, that were incorporated in Northwest Coast art and metal tools. The advent of the fur trade stimulated the tribal economy, generating a demand for carved masks, totem poles, and decorative accessories. However, serious carving was not undertaken by anyone who felt so inclined. Rather, a group of professional craftsmen, who received formal training in an apprenticeship system and were ranked according to their ability, were awarded commissions by the wealthier members of the tribe." Elaborate decoration was encouraged by the importance of gift giving in Northwest Coast culture. To create such work, an array of intricate tools and sturdy axes, originally designed for fishing and cutting down large trees, was refined for use as carving utensils, masks, and effigies. These handsome objects were often decorated with animal figures based on their mythology.

The mythology of the Northwest Coast Indians is filled with totem creatures

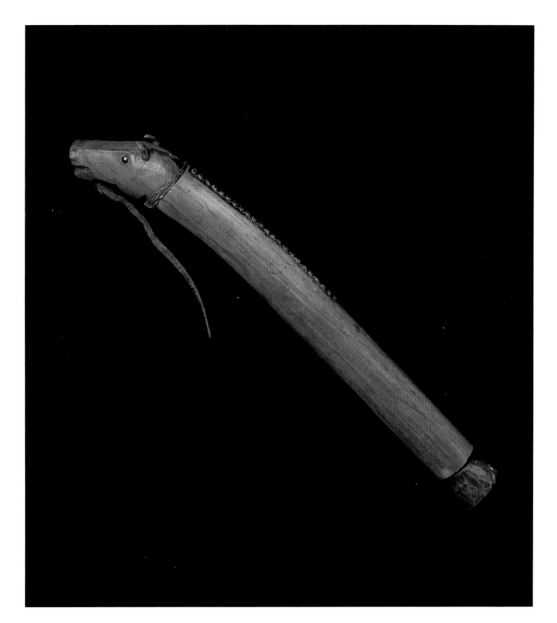

Indian Horse-Dance Stick
Sioux
Wood with metal tacks for
eyes
15″ length
1870s
Courtesy of the Morning Star
Gallery, Santa Fe, N.M.

The horse-dance stick was
carried by men in ceremonial
dances throughout the plains.
Brass upholstery tacks were
so desired for ornamentation
by the Sioux that they were
often traded for furs.

possessing both human and animal characteristics. Whereas the buffalo dominated Plains art, a variety of animals, birds, and fish appear in Northwest Coast art as sources of supernatural power. The largest, the killer whale, was admired for its grace and intelligence. Revered and feared at the same time, it commanded respect for its ambiguous mammal/fish properties. In Indian art, creatures that undergo dramatic transformations often are depicted to underscore their dual roles. Like the whale, the frog was also admired for its aquatic-mammal qualities. Thus the frog is seen imparting his magical properties to the shaman through his tongue.[12] Birds that were equally at ease in the sky or on earth played important artistic roles, as did ducks, who were equally at home in water or in air. Mammals such as otters, bears, wolves, and mountain goats also received attention in Northwest Coast art.

Animals in Native American Art / 225

Painted Hide. Shoshone. Tanned buffalo hide. 42" x 80". c. 1890s.
Wyoming. Courtesy of the Morning Star Gallery, Santa Fe, N.M.

Painted Hide. Cheyenne. Bison leather hide with porcupine quills and ornaments. 63″ x 72″. 1870s. Wyoming. Courtesy of The Denver Art Museum. Photograph: Otto Nelson

Pictorial Parfleche
Anonymous
Painted rawhide
18″ x 12″
c. 1890
Plateau area
Courtesy of the Morning Star
Gallery, Santa Fe, N.M.

The parfleche, shaped like an
envelope adorned with long
side fringes, was a useful
rawhide container that
traveled well. Containing
everything from stored food
to sacred potions, the
parfleche was watertight.
Pictorial images seldom
replaced all-over geometric
designs.

"Indian Boy on Eagle"
E. "Popeye" Reed
(1924–1985)
Tennessee limestone
13″ x 19″ x 11″
Late 1970s
Area around Jackson, Ohio
Private collection
Photography courtesy of the
Phylis Kind Galleries,
Chicago and New York City

Part Irish and part American
Indian, E. "Popeye" Reed
began as an arrowhead carver,
and in the late 1960s became
a serious sculptor. Using
whatever tools were
available, he created a body
of work in limestone and
sandstone encompassing a
wide variety of subjects,
including animals, Indians,
and mythological figures.

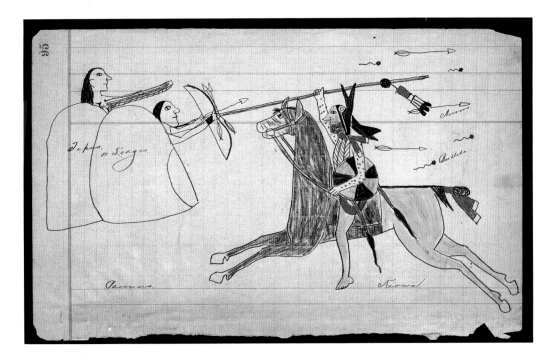

Attacking an Enemy Camp
Plate 47 from *Kiowa
Memories: Images from Indian
Territory, 1880*
Anonymous
Ledger paper
12″ x 7¼″
1880
Oklahoma Territory
Courtesy of the Morning Star
Gallery, Santa Fe, N.M.

A Kiowa warrior with his
horse in full battle attire fends
off the Navajo.

Pawnee Buffalo Hunter
Plate 33 from *Kiowa
Memories: Images from Indian
Territory, 1880*
Anonymous
Ledger paper
12″ x 7½″
1880
Oklahoma Territory
Courtesy of the Morning Star
Gallery, Santa Fe, N.M.

The depiction of game
animals is unusual in Plains
ledger art, which emphasized
military exploits. Here the
buffalo resembles his
ancestors from Paleolithic
cave paintings.

Bear Box
Tlingit
Carved and painted wood,
ornamented with shells
15″ x 12½″ x 7″
Late 19th century
Alaska
Courtesy of the American
Museum of Natural History,
Neg. #2A11271

The elaborate carving of this
box portraying the fearsome
grizzly bear is typical of
many highly decorated
household objects in
Northwest Coast art.

Bear Comb
Tlingit
Carved wood with copper
eyes and bone teeth
Dimensions unavailable
c. 1887
Alaska
Courtesy of the American
Museum of Natural History,
Neg. #321825
Photograph: A. Rota

A shaman's comb worn to
keep the braids and plaits of
hair on top of the head. Here
a bear sits up on its haunches
with a salmon in its forepaws.

Buffalo Fan. "Making Medicine" (1844–1931). Ivory, tempera on silk.
9″ x 17″. c. 1877. St. Augustine, Fla. Courtesy of the Saint Augustine
Historical Society

A member of the Cheyenne tribe, while incarcerated at Fort Marion,
painted this unusual fan as a tourist item for Miss Annie Pidgeon. (In its
dedication to her the artist substituted the Cheyenne word for owl, a hated
symbol, for the word "pidgeon.") It is ironic that the type of narrative
painting usually associated with the brave exploits depicted in hide paintings
and ledger-book art should be reduced to decorating ladies' fans.

LEFT:
Fox-Head Spoon
Anonymous
Carved wood
8″ length
19th century
Midwest
Courtesy of Main Street
Antiques & Art,
West Branch, Iowa

Believed to be of Indian
origin, the carved fox-head
spoon is similar to ladles and
spoons made by various
Plains tribes.

BELOW:
Loon Ladle
Haida
Carved wood
Dimensions unavailable
Late 19th century
Alaska
Courtesy of the American
Museum of Natural History,
Neg. #326935
Photograph: A. Rota

The loon, regarded as a
spirit emissary by members
of Northwest Coast tribes,
appeared frequently in
their art.

Chief's Dance Rattle. Tlingit. Carved and painted wood. Dimensions unavailable. Late 19th century. Alaska. Courtesy of the American Museum of Natural History, Neg. #323380

This rattle is in the shape of a crow. On its back rests the traditional dead man with protruding tongue in the bill of a kingfisher; on the lower side of the bird, and upside down, is an owl with a frog obtaining secrets from it.

Bird Rattle. Nootka. Carved wood. Dimensions unavailable. Late 19th century. West Coast, Vancouver Island. Courtesy of the American Museum of Natural History, Neg. #321822. Photograph: A. Rota

A ceremonial rattle of a bird whose wings are carved in a heart-shaped design.

Bear Painting
Mary Nancy Coloque
Watercolor
14″ x 8″
c. 1960
Jemez Pueblo, New Mexico
Courtesy of the School of
American Research, Santa Fe

A brilliant rendition of the
traditional bear, with a red
heart line surrounded by bear
paws. Since the 1960s the
Jemez Pueblo has produced a
group of outstanding artists.

Coyotes Painting
Ralph Martinez
Watercolor
12¼″ x 7⅝″
20th century
Taos Pueblo, New Mexico
Courtesy of the School of
American Research, Santa Fe

The coyote, a familiar though
unwelcome neighbor in the
Southwest, is infrequently
depicted in folk art.

Twelve Animals. Awa Tsireh. Watercolor. 28¾″ x 22½″. Early
20th century. San Ildefonso Pueblo, New Mexico. Courtesy
of the School of American Research, Santa Fe

Awa Tsireh, one of San Ildefonso's most important artists,
showed promise in this school drawing. Schools providing
materials and encouragement were crucial to the development
of 20th-century Indian easel art.

American Indian Souvenir Pillow. Anonymous. Beadwork. 8¼″
x 8″. 1936. Courtesy of the Ames Gallery of American Folk
Art, Berkeley, Calif.

Souvenir pincushions, pillows, and other beadwork accessories
were made by various tribes for the tourist market starting in
the late 19th century. Birds, horses, and deer appeared more
frequently than the moose pictured here.

Pictorial Rug. Navajo. Handspun yarns. 35″ x 47″. c. 1930. Collected in Cortez, Colo. Courtesy of Joshua Baer & Company, Santa Fe, N.M.

Two horses and their riders face each other in front of the Shiprock, a famous natural rock formation near the Four Corners on the Navajo Reservation in northwestern New Mexico. The white horse is unsaddled and may be a Navajo's horse. The black horse is saddled and his tail has been bobbed, indicating that he might belong to a white man. It appears that the riders have traded horses.

NOTES

The Eighteenth and Nineteenth Centuries

1. Carle Hodge, "Emil Haury, Archeologist," *Arizona Highways,* September 1987, p. 9.
2. Maggie Wilson, "Centennial at Pueblo Grande," *Arizona Highways,* September 1987, p. 25.
3. Alice Morse Earle, *Stage-Coach and Tavern Days* (New York: The Macmillan Company, 1902), p. 140.
4. Ibid., pp. 151–2.
5. Allan I. Ludwig, *Graven Images: New England Stonecarving and Its Symbols, 1650–1815* (Middletown, Conn.: Wesleyan University Press, 1966), p. 296.
6. Myrna Kaye, *Yankee Weathervanes* (New York: E. P. Dutton, 1975), p. 24.
7. Marshall B. Davidson, *The American Heritage History of American Antiques from the Revolution to the Civil War* (New York: American Heritage Publishing Company, 1967), p. 75.
8. Philip M. Isaacson, *The American Eagle* (Boston: Little, Brown, 1975), p. 1.
9. Yvonne Brault Smith, *John Haley Bellamy, Carver of Eagles* (Portsmouth, Me.: Portsmouth Marine Society, 1982), p. x.
10. Davidson, *American Heritage History of American Antiques,* p. 174.
11. Sandra Brant and Elissa Cullman, *Small Folk: A Celebration of Childhood in America* (New York: E. P. Dutton, 1980), p. 127.
12. Jean Lipman and Alice Winchester, *The Flowering of American Folk Art (1776–1876),* (Harmondsworth, Middlesex: Penguin Books, 1977), p. 172.
13. Marshall B. Davidson, ed., *The American Heritage History of Colonial Antiques* (New York: American Heritage Publishing Company, 1967), p. 328.
14. *Lancaster County Historical Society Papers,* vol. XVII, no. 5 (May 3, 1918), p. 86.
15. Rita Susswein Gottesman, comp., *The Arts and Crafts in New York, 1800–1804* (New York: The New-York Historical Society, 1965), p. 442.
16. Alice Winchester, *Versatile Yankee: The Art of Jonathan Fisher, 1768–1847* (Princeton, N.J.: The Pyne Press, 1973), p. 26.
17. Ibid., p. 28.
18. Margaret S. Creighton, *Dogwatch & Liberty Days* (Worcester, Mass.: Peabody Museum of Salem, 1982), p. 54.
19. M. V. Brewington, *Shipcarvers of North America* (New York: Dover Publications, 1962), p. 4.

20. Ibid., p. 8.

21. Charles Levi Woodbury, *The Relation of the Fisheries to the Settlement of North America* (Boston, 1880), p. 26. Cited in Kaye, *Yankee Weathervanes*, p. 50.

22. Cited by Gene and Linda Kangas, "Decoys: Lures for Birds—and Collectors," *The Encyclopedia of Collectibles: Cookware-Detective Fiction* (Alexandria, Va.: Time-Life Books, 1978), p. 130.

23. Marian and Charles Klamkin, *Wood Carvings: North American Folk Sculptures* (New York: Hawthorn Books, 1974), pp. 135–6.

24. Cornelius Weygandt, "Beasts in Dutchland," *The Dutchman* (Summer 1955), p. 12.

25. Dr. Alfred L. Shoemaker, Director of the Pennsylvania Dutch Folklore Center, quoted by Albert I. Drachman in "Tracking the Elusive Distelfink," *The Dutchman* (Summer 1955), p. 28.

26. Earl F. Robacker, "The Peacock," *Pennsylvania Folklife,* vol. 11, no. 1 (Spring 1960), p. 10.

27. Ibid., p. 14.

28. Leah Shanks Gordon, "Chalkware," *Americana,* January 1976, p. 13.

29. Earl F. Robacker, *Touch of the Dutchland* (New York: A. S. Barnes, 1965), p. 134.

30. Tom Kloss, "Wooden Folk Art Carving and Sculpture," *The Old Lancaster Antique Show* (Exhibition catalogue. Lancaster, Pa.: Fulton Press, 1982), p. 45.

31. Cited in Robert Bishop, *American Folk Sculpture* (New York: E. P. Dutton, 1974), p. 204, and Milton E. Flower, *Three Cumberland County Wood Carvers* (Carlisle, Pa.: Cumberland County Historical Society, 1986), p. 6.

32. Milton E. Flower, *Wilhelm Schimmel and Aaron Mountz, Wood Carvers* (Williamsburg, Va.: Abby Aldrich Rockefeller Folk Art Collection, 1965), p. 11.

33. Ibid., p. 6.

34. Bishop, *American Folk Sculpture,* p. 210.

35. John Michael Vlach, *Plain Painters* (Washington and London: Smithsonian Institution Press, 1988), p. 126.

36. Arthur Edwin Bye, "Edward Hicks, 1780–1849," *Bulletin of the Friends Historical Association,* 32 (1943), p. 61.

37. Jane Livingston and John Beardsley, *Black Folk Art in America, 1930–1980* (Exhibition catalogue. Jackson: University of Mississippi Press for the Corcoran Gallery of Art, 1982), p. 26.

38. Ibid., p. 30.

39. R. Thornton, "A Religious Dog," *Wood's Household Magazine,* June 1874, p. 289.

40. Heritage Plantation of Sandwich, *Canines & Felines: Dogs and Cats in American Art* (Exhibition catalogue. Sandwich, Mass.: Heritage Plantation of Sandwich, 1988), p. 5.

THE TWENTIETH CENTURY

1. Charles G. Zug III, with Quincy Scarborough, Mary Anne McDonald, and Neal Conoley, Jr., *Five North Carolina Folk Artists* (Chapel Hill, N.C.: Ackland Art Museum, 1986), p. 66.

2. Ibid., p. 68.

3. Lowery S. Sims, *Bill Traylor: People, Animals, Events* (Exhibition catalogue. New York: Vanderwoude Tananbaum, 1982), unpaged.

4. Quoted from a letter by Robert Cargo to the author, February 9, 1989.

5. Ibid.

6. Cited in a letter from Robert Cargo to the author, February 9, 1989.

7. Quoted in *The Christian Science Monitor,* July 23, 1980.

8. Cited in Judith Alexander, *Nellie Mae Rowe: Visionary Artist* (Exhibition catalogue. Atlanta, Ga.: Southern Arts Federation, 1983), p. 11.

9. Jane Livingston and John Beardsley, *Black Folk Art in America, 1930–1980* (Exhibition catalogue. Jackson: University of Mississippi Press for the Corcoran Gallery of Art, 1982), p. 65.

10. Cited in Jay Johnson and William Ketchum, Jr., *American Folk Art of the Twentieth Century* (New York: Rizzoli Publications, 1983), p. 37.

11. University Art Museum, *Baking in the Sun: Visionary Images from the South* (Exhibition catalogue. Lafayette, La.: University Art Museum, 1987), p. 20.

12. John Michael Vlach, "From Gravestone to Miracle: Traditional Perspective and the Work of William Edmondson," *William Edmondson: A Retrospective*, edited by Georganne Fletcher (Exhibition catalogue. Nashville: Tennessee State Museum, 1981), p. 23.

13. Edmund L. Fuller, *Visions in Stone: The Sculpture of William Edmondson* (Pittsburgh: University of Pittsburgh Press, 1973), p. 16.

14. Ibid., p. 3.

15. Louise LeQuire, *William Edmondson: A Retrospective*, p. 45.

16. Julie Hall, *The Sculpture of Fred Alten* (Exhibition catalogue. Michigan Artrain, 1978), p. 15.

17. Quoted by Robert Merritt in Richmond *Times-Dispatch*, May 10, 1982.

18. Quoted by Elinor Lander Horwitz in *Contemporary American Folk Artists* (Philadelphia and New York: J. B. Lippincott, 1975) pp. 76–7.

19. Jann Malone, "Beneath the Bark," *Country Magazine*, April 1982, p. 39.

20. Zug, et al., *Five North Carolina Folk Artists*, p. 66.

21. Ibid., p. 68.

22. Quoted by Jay Johnson and William Ketchum, Jr., in *American Folk Art of the Twentieth Century*, p. 2.

23. Felipe Archuleta quoted in *Lions and Tigers and Bears, Oh My!* (Exhibition catalogue. Corpus Christi: Art Museum of South Texas, 1986), p. 15.

24. *New Art Examiner*, October 1986, p. 25.

25. Kurt C. Dewhurst and Marsha MacDowell, *Cast in Clay: The Folk Pottery of Grand Ledge, Michigan* (East Lansing: The Museum, Michigan State University, in cooperation with the Grand Ledge Historical Society, 1980), p. 39.

26. Ibid., p. 37.

27. Ibid., p. 39.

ANIMALS IN NATIVE AMERICAN ART

1. J. J. Brody, *Mimbres Pottery: Ancient Art of the American Southwest* (New York: Hudson Hills Press, 1983), p. 15.

2. Charles Avery Amsden, *An Analysis of Hohokam Pottery Design* (Medallion Papers, no. 23. Globe, Ariz.: Gila Pueblo, 1936), p. 44.

3. Lansing B. Bloom, ed., "Bourke on the Southwest," *New Mexico Historical Review*, vol. 13, no. 2 (April 1938), p. 228, cited in Clara Lee Tanner, *Southwest Indian Painting: A Changing Art* (2nd edn. Tucson: University of Arizona Press, 1980), p. 48.

4. David S. Brose, James A. Brown, and David W. Penney, *Ancient Art of the American Woodland Indians* (New York: Harry N. Abrams, in association with the Detroit Institute of Arts, 1985), p. 192.

5. Paul Radin, *The Winnebago Tribe* (New York: Johnson Reprint Corporation, 1970), p. 270.

6. Ibid., pp. 194–5.

7. Walter McClintock, *Old Indian Trails* (London: Constable, 1923), p. 275, cited in Ian M. West, "Plains Indian Horse Sticks," *American Indian Art Magazine* (Spring 1978), p. 62.

8. Maximilian, Prince of Wied, "Travels in the Interior of North America, 1832–1834, Part 2," Vol. 23 in *Early Western Travels, 1746–1846*, edited by R. G. Thwaites (Cleveland: A. H. Clark Co., 1906), p. 102.

9. Alfred J. Miller, *Braves and Buffalo: Plains Indian Life in 1837—Water-colours of Alfred J. Miller with descriptive notes by the artist* (Toronto: University of Toronto Press, 1973), p. 62.

10. James H. Howard, "The Plains-Ojibwa or Bungi," *Anthropological Papers*, 1 (1965a), W. H. Over Museum, Vermillion, S.D., p. 10.

11. Norman Feder, *Two Hundred Years of North American Indian Art* (New York: Frederick Praeger, 1971), p. 6.

12. Peter T. and Jill L. Furst, *North American Indian Art* (New York: Rizzoli International Publications, 1982), p. 15.

Rabbit Painting. Signed on reverse "B. B. Franklin". Oil on board.
12″ x 18″. Dated July 27, 1880. Courtesy of Fredric I. Thaler, Cornwall
Bridge, Conn.

SELECT BIBLIOGRAPHY

Alexander, Judith. *Nellie Mae Rowe* (Exhibition catalogue). Atlanta, Ga.: The Southern Arts Foundation, 1983.

Art Museum of South Texas (Exhibition catalogue). *Lions and Tigers and Bears, Oh My! New Mexican Folk Carvings.* Corpus Christi: Art Museum of South Texas, 1986.

Barret, Richard Carter. *Bennington Pottery and Porcelain.* New York: Crown Publishers, 1958.

Bishop, Robert. *American Folk Sculpture.* New York: E. P. Dutton, 1974.

———. *Folk Painters of America.* New York: E. P. Dutton, 1979.

———, Weissman, Judith Reiter; McManus, Michael; and Nieman, Henry. *Folk Art: Paintings, Sculpture, and Country Objects. The Knopf Collectors' Guides to American Antiques.* New York: Alfred A. Knopf, 1983.

Black, Mary, and Lipman, Jean. *American Folk Painting.* New York: Clarkson Potter, 1966.

Brewington, M. V. *Shipcarvers of North America.* New York: Dover Publications, 1962.

Brody, J. J. *Mimbres Pottery: Ancient Art of the American Southwest.* New York: Hudson Hills Press, 1983.

Brose, David S.; Brown, James A.; and Penney, David W. *Ancient Art of the American Woodland Indians.* New York: Harry N. Abrams, in association with the Detroit Institute of Arts, 1985.

Bye, Arthur Edwin. "Edward Hicks, 1780–1849." *Bulletin of the Friends Historical Association,* 32, (1943).

Carpenter, Miles B. *Cutting the Mustard.* Tappahannock, Va.: American Folk Art Company, 1982.

Chase, Mary Ellen. *Jonathan Fisher: Maine Parson, 1767–1847.* New York: The Macmillan Company, 1948.

Christensen, Erwin O. *Early American Wood Carving.* Cleveland: World Publishing Co., 1952.

Coe, Ralph T. *Sacred Circles: Two Thousand Years of North American Indian Art* (Exhibition catalogue). Kansas City, Mo.: Nelson Gallery of Art—Atkins Museum of Fine Arts, 1977.

Conn, Richard. *Native American Art in the Denver Art Museum.* Seattle: University of Washington Press, 1979.

Davidson, Marshall B., ed. *The American Heritage History of Colonial Antiques.* New York: American Heritage Publishing Co., 1967.

_____. *The American Heritage History of American Antiques from the Revolution to the Civil War.* New York: American Heritage Publishing Co., 1967.

Decordova Museum. *Folk Sculpture from the Collection of Mr. and Mrs. Francis Andrews* (Exhibition catalogue). Lincoln, Mass.: Decordova Museum, 1978.

Dewhurst, Kurt C. *Grand Ledge Folk Pottery.* Ann Arbor: University of Michigan Research Press, 1986.

Dewhurst, Kurt C., and Macdowell, Marsha. *Cast in Clay: The Folk Pottery of Grand Ledge, Michigan.* East Lansing: The Museum, Michigan State University, in cooperation with the Grand Ledge Historical Society, 1980.

Duval, Francis, and Rigby, Ivan B. *Early American Gravestone Art in Photographs.* New York: Dover Publications, 1978.

Earle, Alice Morse. *Stage-Coach and Tavern Days.* New York: The Macmillan Company, 1902.

Earnest, Adele. *The Art of the Decoy.* New York: Clarkson Potter, 1965.

Eaton, Allen H. *Handicrafts of the Southern Highlands.* New York: Dover Publications, 1973.

Everson Museum of Art. *The Animal Kingdom in American Art* (Exhibition catalogue). Syracuse, N.Y.: Everson Museum of Art, 1978.

Ewers, John C. "The Awesome Bear in Plains Indian Art." *American Indian Art Magazine* (Summer 1982), in Feder, Norman, ed., *American Indian Art.* New York: Harry N. Abrams, 1969.

_____. *Plains Indian Sculpture.* Washington, D.C.: Smithsonian Institution Press, 1986.

Finore, Diane. "Art by Bill Traylor." *The Clarion* (Spring–Summer 1983), pp. 42–48.

Fletcher, Georganne, ed. *William Edmondson: A Retrospective* (Exhibition catalogue). Nashville, Tennessee State Museum, 1981.

Flower, Milton E. *Wilhelm Schimmel and Aaron Mountz, Wood Carvers.* Williamsburg, Va.: Abby Aldrich Rockefeller Folk Art Collection, 1965.

_____. *Three Cumberland County Wood Carvers.* Carlisle, Pa.: Cumberland County Historical Society, 1986.

Ford, Alice. *Edward Hicks, Painter of the Peaceable Kingdom.* Philadelphia: University of Pennsylvania Press, 1952.

Fritz, Ronald J. *Michigan's Master Carver Oscar W. Peterson.* Boulder Junction, Wis.: Aardvark Publications, 1987.

Fuller, Edmund L. *Visions in Stone: The Sculpture of William Edmondson.* Pittsburgh: University of Pittsburgh Press, 1973.

Furst, Peter T., and Furst, Jill L. *North American Indian Art.* New York: Rizzoli International Publications, 1982.

God, Man and the Devil: Religion in Recent Kentucky Folk Art (Exhibition catalogue). Lexington: Folk Art Society of Kentucky, 1984.

Gordon, Leah Shanks. "Chalkware." *Americana,* January 1976, pp. 10–13.

Gottesman, Rita Susswein. *The Arts and Crafts in New York, 1800–1804.* New York: The New-York Historical Society, 1965.

Guilland, Harold F. *Early American Folk Pottery.* Philadelphia: Chilton Book Company, 1971.

Hall, Julie. *The Sculpture of Fred Alten* (Exhibition catalogue). N.p., Michigan Artrain, 1978.

The Heart of Creation: The Art of Martin Ramirez (Exhibition catalogue). Philadelphia: Moore College of Art, 1985.

Hemphill, Herbert W., Jr., and Weissman, Julia. *Twentieth Century American Folk Art and Artists.* New York: E. P. Dutton, 1974.

Heritage Plantation of Sandwich. *Canines & Felines: Dogs and Cats in American Art* (Exhibition catalogue). Sandwich, Mass.: Heritage Plantation of Sandwich, 1988.

Isaacson, Phillip M. *The American Eagle.* Boston: Little, Brown, 1975.

Johnson, Jay, and Ketchum, William, Jr. *American Folk Art of the Twentieth Century.* New York: Rizzoli International Publications, 1983.

Jones, Suzi, ed. *Webfoots and Bunchgrassers: Folk Art of the Oregon County* (Exhibition catalogue). Salem: Oregon Arts Council, 1980.

Kaye, Myrna. *Yankee Weathervanes.* New York: E. P. Dutton, 1975.

Keene, Catherine A. *At the Sign of the Brass Dog: Passaic County Folk Art* (Exhibition catalogue). Paterson, N.J.: The Passaic County Historical Society, 1987.

Kimball, Art; Kimball, Brad; and Kimball, Scott. *The Fish Decoy.* Boulder Junction, Wis.: Aardvark Publications, 1986.

Klamkin, Marian, and Klamkin, Charles. *Wood Carving: North American Folk Sculptures.* New York: Hawthorn Books, 1974.

Kloss, Tom. "Wooden Folk Art Carving and Sculpture." *The Old Lancaster Antique Show* (Exhibition catalogue). Lancaster, Pa.: Fulton Press, 1982.

Lasansky, Jeannette. *Central Pennsylvania Redware Pottery, 1780–1904.* Lewisburg, Pa.: Union County Oral Traditions Projects, 1979.

Lavitt, Wendy. "American Folk Toys." *The Clarion* (Winter 1981), pp. 42–7.

Little, Nina Fletcher. "J. O. J. Frost, Painter-Historian of Marblehead." *Art in America,* October 1955, pp. 28–33.

Lipman, Jean. *American Primitive Painting.* New York: Dover Publications, 1972 (originally published by Oxford University Press, 1942).

Lichten, Frances. *Folk Art of Rural Pennsylvania.* New York: Charles Scribner's Sons, 1946.

———. "Pennsylvania Dutch Needlework: Where Did the Worker Find Her Patterns?" *The Dutchman* (Spring 1956).

Lipman, Jean, and Armstrong, Tom, eds. *American Folk Painters of Three Centuries.* New York: Hudson Hills Press, in association with the Whitney Museum of American Art, 1980.

Lipman, Jean, and Winchester, Alice. *The Flowering of American Folk Art (1776–1876).* Harmondsworth, Middlesex: Penguin Books, 1977 (originally published by Viking Press, 1974).

Livingston, Jane, and Beardsley, John. *Black Folk Art in America, 1930–1980* (Exhibition catalogue). Corcoran Gallery of Art. Jackson: University of Mississippi Press and the Center for the Study of Southern Culture, 1982.

———. *Hispanic Art in the United States.* New York: Abbeville Press, 1987.

Ludwig, Allan I. *Graven Images: New England Stonecarving and Its Symbols, 1650–1815.* Middletown, Conn.: Wesleyan University Press, 1966.

McConathy, Dale. *Best of Friends: The Dog and Art* (Exhibition catalogue). New York: The Dog Museum of America, 1983.

McCoy, Ronald. *Kiowa Memories: Images from Indian Territory, 1880.* Santa Fe, N.M.: Morningstar Gallery, 1987.

Meyer, Charles R. *Whaling and the Art of Scrimshaw.* New York: David McKay, 1976.

Michigan State University. *Michigan Folk Art: Its Beginnings to 1941* (Exhibition catalogue). East Lansing: Michigan State University, 1976.

Myers, Jane E. *Highlights of the Renfrew Museum* (Exhibition catalogue). Waynesboro, Pa.: Renfrew Museum, 1980.

Museum of American Folk Art. *Ape to Zebra: A Menagerie of New Mexican Woodcarvings, The Animal Carnival Collection of the Museum of American Folk Art* (Exhibition catalogue). New York: Museum of American Folk Art, 1985.

Robacker, Earl Francis. *Touch of the Dutchland.* New York: A. S. Barnes, 1965.

Robacker, Earl F. and Robacker, Ada A. "Discord in the Garden." *Pennsylvania Folklife* (Summer 1969), pp. 2–7.

———. "Flight of the Distelfink." *Pennsylvania Folk Life* (Summer 1971).

Rubin, Cynthia Elyce, ed. *Southern Folk Art.* Birmingham, Ala.: Oxmoor House, 1985.

Simpson, Milt. *Windmill Weights.* Newark, N.J.: Johnson & Simpson, Graphic Designers, in association with the Museum of American Folk Art, New York, 1985.

Smith, Yvonne Brault. *John Haley Bellamy, Carver of Eagles.* Portsmouth, Me.: Portsmouth Marine Society, 1982.

Tanner, Clara Lee. *Southwest Indian Painting: A Changing Art* (2nd edn.). Tucson: University of Arizona Press, 1980.

Terry, George D., and Myers, Lynn Robertson. *Carolina Folk: The Cradle of a Southern Tradition* (Exhibition catalogue). Charleston, S.C.: McKissick Museum, 1985.

Tomlinson, Juliette, ed. *The Paintings and Journal of Joseph Whiting Stock.* Middletown, Conn.: Wesleyan University Press, 1976.

Transmitters: The Isolate Artist in America. Contributions by Elsa Weiner, Marcia Tucker, Richard Flood, Michael and Julie Hall. Philadelphia: Philadelphia College of Art, 1981.

University Art Museum. *Baking in the Sun: Visionary Images from the South* (Exhibition catalogue). Lafayette, La.: University Art Museum, 1987.

Vlach, John Michael. *The Afro-American Tradition in Decorative Arts.* Cleveland: The Cleveland Museum of Art, 1978.

Waingrow, Jeff. *American Wildfowl Decoys.* New York: E. P. Dutton, 1985.

Wasserman, Emily. *Gravestone Designs.* New York: Dover Publications, 1972.

Wiltshire, William, III. *Pottery of the Shenandoah Valley.* New York: E. P. Dutton, 1975.

Winchester, Alice. *Versatile Yankee: The Art of Jonathan Fisher, 1768–1847.* Princeton, N.J.: The Pyne Press, 1973.

Yood, James. "Martin Ramirez: Madness, Authenticity, and the American Dream." *New Art Examiner,* October 1986.

Zug, Charles G., III, with Scarborough, Quincy; McDonald, Mary Anne; and Conoley, Neal, Jr. *Five North Carolina Folk Artists.* Chapel Hill, N.C.: Ackland Art Museum, 1986.